Editor-in-Chief and Founder:
 Lyndon H. LaRouche, Jr.
Editorial Board: *Lyndon H. LaRouche, Jr. , Helga
 Zepp-LaRouche, Robert Ingraham, Tony
 Papert, Gerald Rose, Dennis Small, Jeffrey
 Steinberg, William Wertz*
Co-Editors: *Robert Ingraham, Tony Papert*
Managing Editor: *Nancy Spannaus*
Technology: *Marsha Freeman*
Books: *Katherine Notley*
Ebooks: *Richard Burden*
Graphics: *Alan Yue*
Photos: *Stuart Lewis*
Circulation Manager: *Stanley Ezrol*

INTELLIGENCE DIRECTORS
Counterintelligence: *Jeffrey Steinberg, Michele
 Steinberg*
Economics: *John Hoefle, Marcia Merry Baker,
 Paul Gallagher*
History: *Anton Chaitkin*
Ibero-America: *Dennis Small*
Russia and Eastern Europe: *Rachel Douglas*
United States: *Debra Freeman*

INTERNATIONAL BUREAUS
Bogotá: *Miriam Redondo*
Berlin: *Rainer Apel*
Copenhagen: *Tom Gillesberg*
Houston: *Harley Schlanger*
Lima: *Sara Madueño*
Melbourne: *Robert Barwick*
Mexico City: *Gerardo Castilleja Chávez*
New Delhi: *Ramtanu Maitra*
Paris: *Christine Bierre*
Stockholm: *Ulf Sandmark*
United Nations, N.Y.C.: *Leni Rubinstein*
Washington, D.C.: *William Jones*
Wiesbaden: *Göran Haglund*

ON THE WEB
e-mail: eirns@larouchepub.com
www.larouchepub.com
www.executiveintelligencereview.com
www.larouchepub.com/eiw
Webmaster: *John Sigerson*
Assistant Webmaster: *George Hollis*
Editor, Arabic-language edition: *Hussein Askary*

EIR (ISSN 0273-6314) *is published weekly
(50 issues), by EIR News Service, Inc.,
P.O. Box 17390, Washington, D.C. 20041-0390.
(703) 777-9451*

European Headquarters: E.I.R. GmbH, Postfach
Bahnstrasse 9a, D-65205, Wiesbaden, Germany
Tel: 49-611-73650
Homepage: http://www.eirna.com
e-mail: eirna@eirna.com
Director: Georg Neudecker

Montreal, Canada: 514-461-1557

Denmark: EIR - Danmark, Sankt Knuds Vej 11,
basement left, DK-1903 Frederiksberg, Denmark.
Tel.: +45 35 43 60 40, Fax: +45 35 43 87 57. e-mail:
eirdk@hotmail.com.

Mexico City: EIR, Sor Juana Inés de la Cruz 242-2
Col. Agricultura C.P. 11360
Delegación M. Hidalgo, México D.F.
Tel. (5525) 5318-2301
eirmexico@gmail.com

Canada Post Publication Sales Agreement
#40683579

Postmaster: Send all address changes to *EIR*, P.O.
Box 17390, Washington, D.C. 20041-0390.

Signed articles in *EIR* represent the views of the
authors, and not necessarily those of the Editorial
Board.

Russia, India and China Assume World Leadership

What Is Science?

June 2—Man is making history before our eyes today, from day to day and even hour to hour, as all the various mutual links between Russia, China, and India become ever closer and ever more numerous, drawing in 70 or more nations comprising well over half of humanity,— as Helga Zepp-LaRouche said in her May 31 TASS interview. It's like a chained ring of magnets pulling themselves into ever-closer alignment. Think of the new revival of interest in the Kra Canal linking the South China Sea with the Indian Ocean (through the Gulf of Thailand and the Andaman Sea). In its current incarnation, this is a Lyndon LaRouche and a Japanese project. It will link India with Southeast Asia and China; it will revolutionize these waters. Lyndon LaRouche said it will be one of the greatest achievements in modern history.

On May 31, Chinese Premier Li Keqiang told Asian editors that, "If China and India work together and forge synergy, it will deliver benefits not only to the Chinese and Indian people, but also to Asia and beyond." Referring to India's recent announcement of a trade corridor deal with Iran and Afghanistan, through Iran's Chabahar Port, Li said that China "welcomes" it.

India and China are for the first time cooperating in regard to Tibet, where in the past China has viewed India with particular sensitivity, given the Dalai Lama's presence in India and a sizeable Tibetan community there.

Also on May 31, former Chinese Ambassador to Russia Li Fenglin was speaking at a two-day conference on China-Russia relations in Moscow. He said that the bilateral relationship is at a 400-year high, but China wants an even higher level of trust with Russia.

"I have a feeling that Putin and Xi have a conceptual understanding of how we should work together, but there are problems of understanding in the mid-level," said Ambassador Li, who spoke perfect and idiomatic Russian. "It does not matter that we have different approaches. It's a normal thing for such big and different countries to have different approaches. The main thing is that they do not lead to contradictions."

All this calls to mind why it was that LaRouche PAC leader Kesha Rogers of Houston wisely chose the figure of the late German-American space pioneer Krafft Ehricke to keynote her fight for the revival of the space program. Ehricke's approach is just like that of Lyndon LaRouche, in that it is not the least bit practical, yet it is extremely effective, as has been demonstrated beyond doubt. Ehricke was one of those leaders of space exploration like Konstantin Tsiolkovsky and Hermann Oberth earlier, whose courage and intellect has brought man to new worlds, beyond even what Christopher Columbus did.

Ehricke was a scientist, but his is real science, not the disgusting mathematical substitute for science which is taught in our schools, and which is represented by Obama's degenerate Secretary of Defense Ashton Carter. Carter's phony version of science brought us the F-35 airplane, at probably $200 million apiece, which doesn't work, and will never work.

Krafft, on the other hand, among many other bold feats of science, forecast precisely the 1970 Apollo 13 mission, in a paper written in 1948. Typically for him, his 1948 paper said that it had been written in 2400, looking back 350 years to the first manned Mars mission in 2050, called "Expedition Ares." Terence Norton, the leader of that mission, had had to answer the objection that the limitations on the technologies available in 2050,— principally the availability of only chemical propulsion for space travel,— increased the likelihood of "a departure from the normal schedule," and with it the failure of the mission and even the death of its crew. What was his answer? To cancel the mission? In his report to the "Space Board," he wrote:

"In considering the problem from any viewpoint, the question may arise: In what way may the challenge offered by a departure from the normal schedule be met with the technical resources at hand? Does such not improbable situation offer some chances to bring home the amazing results of human courage; or does a failure to cope with the situation mean certain death somewhere in the depths of space, to all on board?

"A study of the following pages will show that the technical group has increased the safety factor to a figure far higher than that which was considered the maximum when the project was established. The rest can be left to the character and spirit of the party. It is frankly admitted that possible dangers exist which cannot be anticipated, but the group is firmly convinced that courage, resource, and the scientific attainments of those selected to make the voyage, will meet successfully the challenge of space travel." (See *21st Century Science and Technology*, Spring 2003, p. 34)

Another factor was realistic, thorough, and diverse training, training, training,— much of it in space. Note that most of the redundancy built into "Expedition Ares" was identical to that found in the Apollo missions: namely, the clustering of different independently survivable modules, each one both tailored to a specific purpose, but at the same time general-purpose.

And just like Apollo 13, "Expedition Ares" suffered a mishap and a "departure from normal schedule." Like Apollo 13, the mission had to be aborted, but as with Apollo 13, every one of the crewmen was rescued, and made it back alive to Earth.

Kesha Rogers certainly knows what she's talking about.

EIR Contents

www.larouchepub.com Volume 43, Number 24, June 10, 2016

NASA

**Cover
This Week**

*Earthrise, seen
by man for the
first time, taken
from the Moon,
by the Apollo X
mission.*

I. Puppet Obama

PETITION

The Warsaw Summit Prepares for War, It's Time to Leave NATO Now!

May 30—The following appeal is being circulated internationally, including on the websites of the international LaRouche movement.

The upcoming NATO summit in Warsaw on July 8-9, is expected to be yet another provocation against Russia. By signing this call, we say "stop" this nuclear escalation, before the irreparable occurs!

The hour is grave. A new missile crisis is building, in a mirror image of that which led the Soviet Union in 1962 to deploy nuclear warheads in Cuba, at the doorstep of the United States. Today, the situation is the reverse. At the time, NATO was fighting the Warsaw Pact; today, it is organizing a summit in Warsaw!

We the undersigned observe that NATO is carrying out a provocative policy of "encirclement":

1. The continuous eastward expansion of NATO towards the borders of Russia, despite the guarantees given by the West to Gorbachov in 1989 that this would not happen;
2. The deployment of the Aegis anti-missile defense system in Romania, Poland, Turkey, and Spain. These weapons, equipped with MK41 launchers, can be used for defensive missions (air, land, sea), but also for offensive attacks with nuclear weapons;
3. The planned permanent rotational deployment in the Baltic States, Poland, and Romania, of four battalions of 1,000 troops each, and heavy military equipment;
4. The creation of a "Nordic Front" against Russia, comprising an alliance of NATO members Denmark, Iceland, and Norway, and of

NATO's "Partnership for Peace" (Sweden and Finland);
5. The modernization of nuclear weapons, in particular the B61-12 bomb and the Long Range Standoff (LRSO) Cruise Missiles, based in Germany. U.S. Senator Dianne Feinstein said of these weapons: "The so-called improvements to this weapon seemed to be designed ... to make it more usable, to help us fight and win a limited nuclear war."

To put an end to this threat, we demand:

1. That our government adopt a policy of the "empty chair" (boycott) at the next NATO summit in Warsaw;
2. That our government announce its intention to leave NATO, which no longer has any "raison d'être."

To escape the current countdown to nuclear war, we also call on our government to create without delay the conditions for a new global peace and security architecture, based on the win-win cooperation proposed by the BRICS, cooperation which Europe and the United States, in their own interests, should join in.

The vast efforts we deployed in the 20th Century for war, must be mobilized today for peace and mutual development!

Sign here:

https://larouchepac.com/20160530/petition-warsaw-summit-prepares-war-its-time-leave-nato-now

The AfD Party: Old Wine In New Bottles?

PART THREE

by Helga Zepp-LaRouche, chair of the German party
Civil Rights Movement Solidarity *BüSo*

June 3—There is no doubt about it: The majority of the population in Germany feels abandoned, and has the overwhelming impression that the political ruling class is motivated by anything but the pursuit of the general welfare. The decisions of the heartless bureaucrats in Brussels are certainly not transparent. But what people do see is that that the living standards of many have been sinking for about a quarter of a century; that medical care is getting worse; and that if you are among the unfortunate victims of Hartz 4, or are a member of some other such socially powerless group, often you cannot even afford the bare necessities, much less participate in the cultural life of society.

For years on end, there was allegedly no money for the poor or for affordable housing. But then, suddenly, billions of Euros, in the three digits, were made available to "rescue" the banks and speculators, and sums in the double-digit billions were suddenly found "in a coat pocket" for the refugees. "A pretty large coat pocket," people grumble, among themselves. And then there is increasing anxiety over the growing threats—the growing danger of war, the danger of terrorism, lack of understanding of the cultures of immigrants, fear of poverty in old age—the list of problems seen as existential keeps getting longer.

That general feeling of "getting a raw deal," all sorts of resentments, and the outrage of angry citizens are precisely what the *Alternative für Deutschland* (AfD) party, the various Pegida offshoots, and the New Right feed upon. This is not just a spontaneous reflex; behind it lies a specific method. Peter Sloterdijk, with whom

Wikimedia Deutschland

Alternative für Deutschland *"party philosopher" Marc Jongen's guiding light Peter Sloterdijk has written a world history of rage.*

the AfD's "party philosopher" Marc Jongen collaborated for years as an assistant at the Karlsruhe University of Arts and Design, has even written a world history of rage.

Rage as Driver of History?

In a 2006 book, published in English translation in 2010, titled *Rage and Time*, Sloterdijk presents the thesis that rage is one of the driving forces of history. He constructs a theory of history according to which—starting with Greek mythology and the first lines of Homer's *Iliad*—rage is a god-like capability, something like a divinely ordained eruption of power, which is

According to Jongen collaborator Peter Sloterdijk, rage is one of the driving forces of history, starting with Greek mythology. This image from Greek mythology shows Achilles killing Penthisilea. She was helping to defend Troy.

manifested in the form of *thymos*, and is later presented by Plato as one of the three pillars of the human psyche, between reason and passion. Sloterdijk then traces his perspective on history from ancient Greece to the vengeful God of the Judaic world, to the teachings of the Church fathers of the Middle Ages, up to the communist "world bank of rage." The ultimate demand of his book is for the release of "thymotic energy," as if the world hadn't had to endure an overdose of it with the radicalized extremist movements of the Twentieth Century and experienced the historical consequences such negative energy can cause.

If Sloterdijk's bestial image of man were correct, then a human being would be nothing more than an aggressive watchdog that becomes the more effective, the more it is incited and provoked. If rage and resentment were a principal driving force in the history of mankind, then in all likelihood, we would have bashed each other to death in a very early era, possibly in the era of hunting and gathering, when we ate rabbits and berries, and rage over a missed meal would have been vented on our neighbors. Mankind would never have risen mentally above the infantile state in which a spoiled brat kicks his younger brother in the shins to get the toy blocks.

If Friedrich Schiller assumed that Kant must have had a very unhappy childhood to come up with such unfree thoughts as the Categorical Imperative, how absolutely miserable and terrible must the childhood of this misanthrope Sloterdijk have been! Of course, for Sloterdijk, who believes man is only the "king of the domesticated animals," everything that differentiates mankind from the other forms of life is closed off and unreachable—his creativity, his humanity, his receptivity to beauty, his ability to produce great creations of Classical art, his unlimited talent for discovering ever deeper the laws of the physical universe.

No, Sloterdijk's world is no less ugly than the radical biological determinism of a Björn Höcke: In 2010, Sloterdijk spoke of the "fertility in misery" of the Arabs, who used their reproduction rate as a "demographic weapon" against Europe.

Sloterdijk's longstanding assistant Marc Jongen—the current speaker of the AfD in Baden Württemberg and a member of the AfD's national program committee—has adopted several of his ideas, among them his ideology of the history-making function of rage. He says the German population is suffering from a "thymotic deficit," and touts the AfD as the only party which not only addresses the rage and anger in the population, but knows how to spur it on. He calls that "raising the thymos tension"—in other words, riling up the rage in the population. Only in this way, Jongen explains, can we bring people to oppose the "threat" of "mass migration." No wonder that the star of the Pegida demonstration praises Jongen as the "great hope of the movement."

Inciting enraged citizens in this way—inflaming them—is playing with fire. It is the method of demagogues who take up real grievances, only to respond with plausible but catchword-like—and therefore false—arguments. Take an example from Jongen: "Of the hundreds of millions of needy people in the world, we can only bring a very small, nearly infinitesimal percent to Europe. The idea that we in Europe could be responsible for justice in the world as a whole, is an expression of gigantic hubris." The implication of this statement is that because it is a nearly infinitesimal percentage, it makes no significant difference whether we refuse these people (otherwise described as a "mass immigration") entrance into Europe, never mind what happens to them.

painting by Jean Duplessis-Bertaux in 1793

Storming of the royal Tuileries Palace on Aug. 10, 1793, led to the fall of the French monarchy.

thermonuclear world war—which represents the greatest obstacle to the continued existence of the human race.

The only way to overcome all of these existential threats—threats that the AfD wants to exploit for its own ends—lies in overcoming geopolitics and geopolitical strategy once and for all, and establishing a totally new paradigm organized around the common aims of mankind. If we are not able to reach the higher level of reason, the level on which the common interests of a universal humanity are achieved, we will not fare any better than the dinosaurs, whose bodies were impressive, but whose brains were relatively tiny. In any case, the solution to these problems does not lie on the level of poor watchdogs and poor Sloterdijks.

Or Else, the Paradigm of Love

The crux of the matter is this: That this kind of thinking implies that the neoliberal financial dogma which the AfD fully supports—as they recently demonstrated with their trading in gold—is a permanent feature of the world. But in reality, this trans-Atlantic financial system is on the verge of disintegration, and can only be superseded by a complete reorganization of the system, the introduction of a global Glass-Steagall system of banking separation, and the reconstruction of the world economy through the expansion of the New Silk Road. The AfD has no competence in any of these matters. Jongen criticizes the clear lack of "thymotic virtues," once called the "manly virtues," especially in the approach to all things military. These, he says, are at best tolerated as a necessary evil. Jongen concludes: "I have the feeling that our political elite has since 1968 forgotten the very elementary lessons of foreign policy and geopolitics."

The "elementary lessons of geopolitics" are currently being carried out in NATO exercises in Poland, the Baltics states, and Romania, and by U.S. forces in the South China Sea. It is that geostrategy, a remnant from the Nineteenth and Twentieth Centuries, which brought us two World Wars, and has now brought us to the edge of obliterating humanity in a third—this time a global and

Friedrich Schiller's answer to the Jacobin terror of the French Revolution, an example of a rebellion of enraged citizens par excellence—about which he said that a great historical moment had found a little people—was his *Letters on the Aesthetical Education of Man*. In them he stressed that from then on, improvements in the political realm could only be achieved through the ennoblement of the individual—and that meant, above all, educating the emotions up to the level of reason. Gotthold Lessing argued, in a wonderful analysis of the artistic method, with reference to the famous sculpture of Laocoön and His Sons, that the artist can not present pure emotion—in this case, agony—without aesthetic ennoblement, if he is to meet the requirements of Classical art. Rage and anger, as well as hate and envy, belong to the lowest level of human emotions.

If we are to overcome the enormous challenges with which we are confronted today, we can only do so with love,—love for mankind, and love for our own humanity.

This article has been translated from German.

What Obama Really Said At Hiroshima

by Rachel Brinkley, LaRouche PAC Policy Committee, Boston

June 6—While media reports about President Barack Obama's speech in Hiroshima may have noted that Obama did not apologize for the United States having dropped two atomic bombs on Japan in 1945, none of those reports came close to accurately covering what he actually said there.

The important point is not that he didn't apologize, but that he put forth an argument consciously designed to dishearten mankind about itself, so that any future act of war would not be resisted by a demoralized population. In so doing, he prepared the way for the nuclear war that he is provoking. From far down below, Bertrand Russell is gloating over this U.S. President's adherence to his own Satanic doctrine, put forward at the beginning of the last century.

Listen to Obama's actual words at Hiroshima:

It is not the fact of war that sets Hiroshima apart. Artifacts tell us that violent conflict appeared with the very first man. Our early ancestors, having learned to make blades from flint and spears from wood, used these tools not just for hunting, but against their own kind. On every continent, the history of civilization is filled with war, whether driven by scarcity of grain or hunger for gold, compelled by nationalist fervor or religious zeal.…

The world war that reached its brutal end in Hiroshima and Nagasaki was fought among the wealthiest and most powerful of nations. Their civilizations had given the world great cities and magnificent art. Their thinkers had advanced ideas of justice and harmony and truth. And yet the war grew out of the same base instinct for domination or conquest that had caused conflicts among the simplest tribes, an old pattern amplified by new capabilities and without new constraints.

Obama proclaims that mankind is programmed to kill, and then repeats the Russellite dogma that science, rather than being an integral part of a developing mankind, has resulted simply in the ability to kill larger numbers of people all at once.

He lies blatantly on the issue of his own nuclear weapons policy, saying, "But among those nations like my own that hold nuclear stockpiles, we must have the courage to escape the logic of fear and pursue a world without them." This, while the United States is upgrading its own nuclear arsenal to the tune of $1 trillion, including supplying a new B61-12 tail-kit that allows existing bombs to be directed hundreds of miles further into enemy territory, essentially creating an entirely new class of thermonuclear weapons.

'The Necessity of Killing'

Obama's belief that power lies in killing, was

Lord Bertrand Russell

UN

clearly revealed by his own speech writer, Ben Rhodes, in a recent *New York Times Magazine* article. Rhodes declared that Obama's drone policy is a result of his childhood in Indonesia, which put him in close proximity to the 1965-66 massacre of a half million to a million Indonesians—when his "interaction at that time with power was very intimate." Obama's policy, he said, is one "which understands the hard and at times absolute necessity of killing," unlike other American leaders.

The truth about what Obama actually said in Hiroshima, was further underscored last week when the Indonesian Defense Minister, Gen. Ryamizard Ryacudu, cited Obama's words as justification for that Indonesian massacre itself. After noting that Obama had not apologized, Gen. Ryacudu explained that "Millions of people died because of the bomb, and that was war," and then perpetuated the lie that those killed in the 1960s massacre had mounted an "uprising," so that the victims "deserved to die."

Let's be clear: Dropping the bombs on Hiroshima and Nagasaki was an unnecessary massacre of innocent civilians, as the Japanese had been successfully hemmed in and cut off from their supply lines by Gen.

creative commons/Ari Levinson

In Hiroshima Obama revealed his conception of mankind by explaining away geopolitical wars, including his own, as growing out of a base human instinct that is inescapable.

MacArthur, and were already negotiating to surrender. Not only does Obama not regret such senseless acts of murder, but he narcissistically believes that they are necessary and justified. Obama is a killer. He is killing now, and he will kill again. He must be removed from office before the next kill occurs, which could end the human race in a few hours.

Lyndon LaRouche emphasized, to an audience in Manhattan on June 4, what must be done:

> The first thing you have to do is get rid of Obama. That's a good starting point: throw him out. Throw him out of all offices. Look, the guy's a madman; he's a mass murderer. He has been on record, a man who killed people in great numbers, on Tuesdays. And is probably still doing it. Everything about Obama is Satanic, and those who worship and support Obama, such as we have with a couple of Presidential candidates here—they're not qualified to function, that is, for any social purposes, and that's the point.

> The year 2017 is much too late. Act now or there might not be another chance—Obama must be thrown out.

Unsurvivable

A dark, gruesome, but wholly true depiction of the threat of thermonuclear war, its consequences, and Obama's deployment of a major portion of the U.S. thermonuclear capabilities in multiple theaters threatening both Russia and China.

http://larouchepac.com/unsurvivable

British Empire Behind Coup in Brazil

by Cynthia R. Rush

June 1—For at least a year, establishment media in Brazil, the United States and Europe have published one article after another, singing the praises of the *Lava Jato* (Operation Car Wash) investigation into bribery and corruption in Brazil, involving the state oil firm Petrobras, major national construction and engineering companies such as Odebrecht, and President Dilma Rousseff, or "Dilma" as she is known in and beyond Brazil, who was impeached on May 12 and forced to step down to stand trial on charges of "administrative malfeasance." Sensationalist headlines scream of "massive corruption," payoffs, and money-laundering uncovered by *Lava Jato*, and the "culture of impunity" that let politicians, legislators, and businessmen off the hook. Aggressive young prosecutors and judges are hailed as heroes for fighting to restore "democracy" to Brazil.

All of these developments have been portrayed by the international media as internal, "compartmentalized" political developments in Brazil. In truth, however, the impeachment of President Dilma Rousseff, as well as the actions taken against former Argentine President Cristina Fernández de Kirchner, and the determination to extinguish the patriotic nation-building forces in those two nations, must be viewed within the context of the pre-war mobilization now fully unfurled by the trans-Atlantic alliance of the Obama administration and the British Empire he serves. In addition to the destruction of the people of Argentina and Brazil, it is China and Russia who are the targets of London and Washington: Everything that is happening must be understood in the context of the NATO build-up in Eastern Europe and the U.S. provocations against China in East Asia. This is all a prelude to global war.

'Clean Hands' in Brazil

Be clear on this. There is no "democratic" revolution taking place in Brazil. This is an international bankers' coup, a "color revolution," ordered by the British Empire with one goal: to plunge Brazil into un-

Casa Rosada Presidencia de la nación Argentina

Brazil's President Dilma Rousseff (left) and Argentine President Cristina Fernández at the Argentine Presidential residence on Feb. 4, 2012.

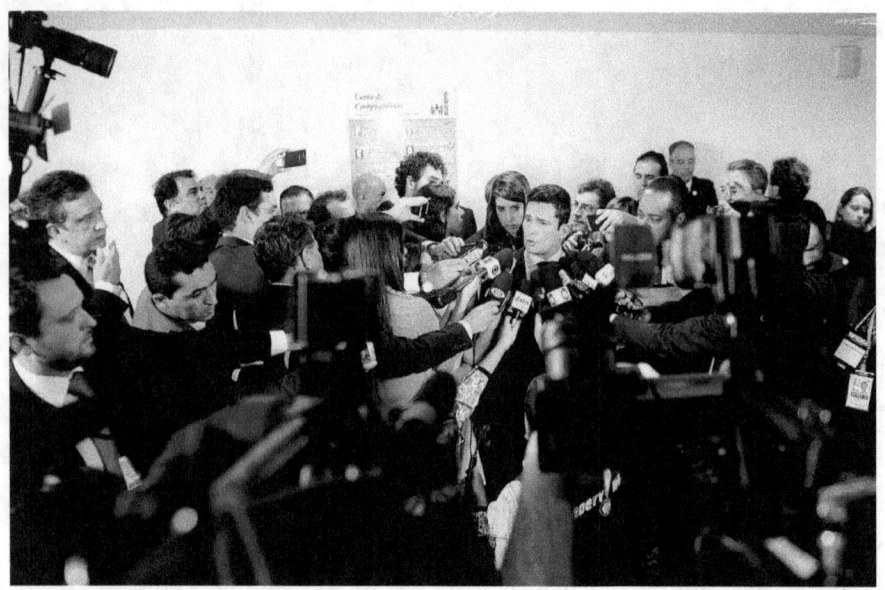
Agencia senado

Brazilian Federal Judge Sergio Moro ran the coup operation against President Dilma Rousseff on behalf of London and Wall Street, and was in constant touch with the FBI and the Department of Justice of the Obama Administration.

cle, "Considerations on Operation Clean Hands." He is in constant touch with the FBI and the U.S. Department of Justice (DOJ).

According to sources cited by the May 21 edition of Brazil's *Estadão*, the DOJ maintains "constant contact" with Brazilian legal authorities "in search of information about corruption, and also to collaborate with Brazilian investigations."

Argentina's Role

Lava Jato began to operate in Brazil as early as late 2014, just after Dilma was elected to a second term, defeating Wall Street's candidate Aecio Neves in November of that year. But it was the election of hard-core monetarist Mauricio Macri in neighboring Argentina last November, and his own announced economic and foreign policy shift toward an alliance with the United States, that emboldened *Lava Jato*'s operatives to go into high gear, knowing they could count on Macri's support. As soon as he took office in December, Macri immediately began to reverse the nationalist policies of his predecessor Cristina Fernández de Kirchner and let the Obama administration know that he would be an entirely trustworthy ally.

It was Macri and Obama who responded to Dilma's impeachment with almost identical statements, saying that Brazil's "institutional process" must be respected and allowed to play out, no matter the outcome. That stood in stark contrast to the regional Unasur organization, the Organization of American States, and other governments, which charged that the impeachment violated the rule of law.

One of Macri's first acts in office—indicating where his loyalties lie—was to make a deal with the vulture funds that had preyed on Argentina for more than a decade and whose demands Fernández and her late husband and predecessor, Néstor Kirchner, had ignored. Under investigation for his and his family's murky offshore business activities, as revealed in the Panama Papers, and challenged on his public defense of the Queen's drug bank HSBC, which is under indictment, Macri has launched his own *mani pulite* witch-hunt

governability that will be felt in the rest of South America, force it out of the BRICS or diminish its role there, and "realign" it with Obama's Washington and the corpse of the trans-Atlantic financial system. Interim President Michel Temer and his Foreign Minister José Serra, whose government is fragile at best, have already sworn fealty to Obama's insane policy outlook, preparing to scuttle the Mercosur customs union and embrace the Trans-Pacific Partnership (TPP) to advance Washington's free trade agenda.

There never was any evidence to justify Dilma's impeachment, other than that British imperial interests require Brazil's destabilization—it's the seventh largest economy in the world, with immense natural and human resources—to achieve their geopolitical goals. The majority of the senators who "voted their conscience" for Dilma's impeachment, are themselves under investigation on charges stemming from *Lava Jato*, or past misdeeds.

The *modus operandi* of choice here is the same *mani pulite* or "Clean Hands" operation deployed against Italy in the 1990s to dismantle its national institutions and facilitate the country's takeover by British-directed financial speculators. The State Department-trained judge running *Lava Jato*, Sergio Moro, who is even being mooted as a future presidential candidate, has publicly stated that he is following the *mani pulite* "model," which he favorably evaluated in a 2004 arti-

against the still very popular former President, using an allied faction of the judiciary to charge her, her family, and political allies with embezzlement, money-laundering, and fraud in hopes of jailing her.

The Macri-owned judge Claudio Bonadio has already indicted Fernández in one case, but others are expected to follow. On May 19, the London *Financial Times* quoted an executive from the New York-based Eurasia Group lamenting that Argentina lacked the ability to carry out "a serious and extensive investigation" of the kind *Lava Jato* is doing in Brazil.

In discussion with his associates May 12, the day Dilma was impeached, *EIR* Founding Editor Lyndon LaRouche warned that if the British Empire doesn't achieve its goals through coups or by jailing Dilma and Cristina Fernández on criminal charges, it will resort to assassination.

It's the British, Stupid

Dilma is correct in asserting that she is the victim of a coup, but errs in identifying its authors as only her domestic political enemies—although she undoubtedly knows otherwise. British paw-prints are all over Brazil's destabilization. At its heart, find the London-steered Obama administration, its DOJ, and the FBI, which have been running the *Lava Jato* dragnet from the get-go, coordinating directly with U.S.-trained, local "anti-fraud" prosecutors, to establish a government of, for, and by speculative vulture and hedge funds.

Add to this that the leaders of the "social movements" organizing this color revolution, such as the Free Brazil Movement (MBL), are Margaret Thatcher-loving proponents of the British Empire's fascist "Austrian School of Economics" associated with the infamous Friedrich von Hayek. The Austrian School's Atlas

The sign "less Marx, more Mises" at a demonstration against President Rousseff in Brazil, was sponsored by the British empire's fascist Austrian School of Economics.

The Koch brothers financed the training of many of the "social movements" that were used to carry out the color revolution in Brazil.

mises.org

Agencia Brazil

Foundation—generously financed by the U.S. Koch brothers, the neocon billionaire oil magnates—reported last year that many MBL members "have passed through Atlas Network's premier training program, the Atlas Leadership Academy, and are now applying what they learned on the ground."

The MBL, which has dominated the anti-government marches in São Paulo this year, the center of the opposition nationally, is one of an array of Koch-financed entities—including the Institute for Humane Studies and Students for Liberty—that make up the anti-government shock troops. Brazil's Ludwig von

Mises Institute was ecstatic with the release of 10,000 balloons with the slogan "Less Marx, More Mises," at one of the anti-Dilma demonstrations in São Paulo.

While these hit squads were amping up the anti-Dilma witch-hunt on the streets, Arminio Fraga—former executive at the Quantum Fund founded by British agent and global drug-legalizer George Soros—was maneuvering behind the scenes to ensure that the right Wall Street-vetted individuals were brought into the shaky "National Salvation" government of Michel Temer, who is not only hated, but is also under investigation by *Lava Jato*, as is half his cabinet.

Fraga has already given his stamp of approval to the "dream team," as Goldman Sachs called it, put together by Finance Minister Henrique Meirelles, formerly of FleetBoston Global Bank, who has been given special powers to impose the draconian economic policy demanded by London and Wall Street, starting with cutting pensions, reducing workers' rights, and social programs. The social explosion to follow will further Brazil's descent into chaos.

Rounding out the picture is the role of the powerful *Rede Globo* media network, which used its significant clout to spread lies and slanders against Dilma, declaring her guilty and demanding her removal. *EIR* has previously documented Rede Globo's ties to the highest levels of British imperial interests, including its links to depopulation fanatics, the World Wide Fund for Nature (World Wildlife Foundation), founded by Royal Consort Prince Philip and Prince Bernhard of Holland, a full-fledged member of the Nazi Party.

Former Argentine President Néstor Carlos Kirchner (right) at a Nov. 4, 2005 press conference in Argentina. Kirchner and then-president of Brazil Lula da Silva crushed President George W. Bush's attempt to impose a Free Trade Area of the Americas.

Taking the 'B' Out of the BRICS

Regime change in Brazil is intended to usher in an era of fascist coups in Ibero-America with the accompanying London- and Wall Street-directed free trade policies to carry out the British Empire's policies of depopulation and economic destruction.

In 2005, at the Americas Summit held in Mar del Plata, Argentina, then President Néstor Kirchner and his Brazilian counterpart Inácio Lula da Silva crushed George W. Bush when he proposed that member nations adopt the Free Trade Area of the Americas (FTAA) for Ibero-America. Bush was humiliated and the FTAA never went anywhere.

Now the goal is to impose some updated version of the failed Bush scheme on the entire continent. To achieve that, imperial financial interests have to take the "B" out of the BRICS, by plunging Brazil into insti-

tutional chaos and wiping out its advanced scientific and technological capabilities which, like Argentina's, are vital to both national and regional development, particularly in the context of the BRICS paradigm.

The BRICS dynamic in Ibero-America really came to life at the July 2014 BRICS annual summit in Fortaleza, Brazil, hosted by Rousseff. There, almost all the nations of South and Central America and the Caribbean, through their representative regional organizations (the Union of South American Nations, Unasur; the Common Market of the South, Mercosur; and the Community of Latin American and Caribbean States, Celac), embraced the BRICS, seeing in its New Development Bank and the offers of Chinese President Xi Jinping and Russian President Vladimir Putin for cooperation in physical economic development, a real alternative to the austerity and "green" agenda offered by

creative commons

The BRICS dynamic surged forward at the July, 2014 BRICS annual summit in Fortaleza, Brazil. The five BRICS heads of state at that summit are shown here (left to right): Russian President Vladimir Putin, Prime Minister of India Narendra Modi, Brazil President Dilma Rousseff, China President Xi Jinping, South African President Jacob Zuma.

the Obama administration, the World Bank, and the IMF.

Before and after that summit, Xi, Putin, and Chinese Premier Li Keqiang toured several nations of the region separately and signed important agreements, including for financing—several of them for major infrastructure projects in the areas of nuclear energy, transportation, manufacturing, communications, and technology transfer. Two of the mega-projects put on the table—which inspired great enthusiasm because of their potential to transform the entire region—are the Nicaraguan Grand Interoceanic Canal and the proposed transoceanic railroad from Brazil to Peru, including possibly a route going through Bolivia.

Plea Bargain Heaven

It was to destroy this win-win perspective that *Lava Jato* was put into motion, with direct coordination between the U.S. DOJ, the FBI, and Judge Moro and his team of young, hotshot prosecutors, several of them trained at Harvard.

Moro isn't just any ambitious judge. In 2007, at the urging of then U.S. Ambassador to Brazil, Clifford Sobel, Moro was granted a "scholarship" to spend three weeks in the United States, which included a training program at the State Department. Sobel, previously a managing partner and founder of the Valor Capital Group in New York and Brazil, was very well connected to international financier circles. Condoleezza Rice ran the State Department at that time under President George W. Bush, whose economic policies were no different than those espoused today by the Atlas Foundation's shock troops in the streets of São Paulo—and by the Obama administration.

Aside from boasting that he has modeled his witchhunt on *mani pulite*, Moro praises the virtues of the FBI's plea bargain system, which for *Lava Jato* is the centerpiece of its *modus operandi*. Using pre-trial arrests of targets to extract plea bargains, and selective passing of innuendos and information extracted in the plea bargains to major media, what started out as an attack on Petrobras now has 230 Brazilian companies and an untold number of politicians as its targets. No banks or hedge funds have been touched!

The FBI and DOJ justify their central role in *Lava Jato* by using the pretext of the U.S. Foreign Corrupt Practices Act (FCPA), which states that any foreign company that issues bonds in the U.S. market can be investigated or monitored. Carlos Fernando dos Santos Lima, a Cornell University-educated member of the prosecutorial team working under Moro in the city of Curitiba in Paraná state, bragged to Reuters in November 2014 that Brazilian prosecutors had been coordinating "for months" with the DOJ, the U.S. Securities and Exchange Commission (SEC), and the FBI. That was less than a month after Dilma Rousseff was re-elected President, impeding, for the moment, the all-out attack on Brazil.

By August 2015, a decisive meeting was held involving the lawyer for jailed money-launderer Alberto Youssef, who arranged a plea bargain with *Lava Jato* prosecutors in exchange for providing information. In the meeting were an FBI agent, but also representatives

Jailed money launderer Alberto Yousseff made a plea bargain agreement with U.S. officials, worked out by the FBI, the U.S. DOJ, and U.S. and British hedge funds, which provided "information" that was used to impeach President Rousseff.

of U.S. and British hedge and pension funds that had filed class action suits against Petrobras, in hopes of winning billions for alleged "losses" resulting from the corruption scheme! It was agreed at that August meeting that Youssef would sign a plea-bargain with U.S.—not Brazilian—officials.

On September 22, Youssef's lawyer, Antonio Figueiredo Basto, flew to the United States to work out specific terms for his client's "cooperation" with the FBI and DOJ.

In that meeting it was arranged that Patrick Stokes, then head of the FCPA unit at the DOJ (now Senior Deputy Chief of Fraud), would travel personally to Curitiba in October or November, to meet *for four days* with Judge Moro, his prosecutorial team, and Youssef, on where the *Lava Jato* case could go next. That October, the head of the Brazilian Chamber of Deputies, Edwardo Cunha, himself a target of *Lava Jato*, announced that he was initiating impeachment proceedings against Rousseff.

The continuing FBI role in the case is so flagrant, that George "Ren" McEachern, head of the FBI's Washington Field Office International Corruption Squad, was just in Brazil two weeks ago, where he was the featured speaker at the May 17-18 "Fourth Anti-Corruption Congress" in São Paulo, organized by Thomson Reuters and the LEC (Legal, Ethics, Compliance) company. Billed as the biggest "business compliance" meeting in Latin America, *Lava Jato* was its big theme this year.

It is also relevant that the DOJ and FBI both recently offered to Argentine Justice Minister Germán Garavano their expert assistance in "clarifying" two cases in which Macri-allied prosecutors and judges have tried to implicate Cristina: the 1994 bombing of the AMIA Jewish social center, blamed on Iran, and the suspicious January 2015 death of federal prosecutor Alberto Nisman, who had been investigating Cristina for the alleged coverup of the Iranian role in the AMIA bombing.

On Jan. 20, 2015 Nisman was scheduled to present to Congress a flimsy dossier he had concocted of supposed evidence that Cristina Fernández had covered up Iran's role in the AMIA bombing, but he was killed one day before his scheduled appearance. Immediately, media that speak for Wall Street and London, both inside Argentina and internationally, put out the word that Cristina was implicated, even though three different federal judges subsequently threw Nisman's dossier out of court for lack of evidence.

Economic Destruction

So far, the *Lava Jato* wrecking ball has succeeded in paralyzing Brazil's economy, particularly targeting those scientific and high-technology capabilities so fundamental for physical-economic development, while putting an estimated two million people out of work in 2015. It has placed the father of Brazil's nuclear program, Admiral Othon Luiz Pinheiro da Silva, under house arrest for corruption, and threatens the continued existence of oil giant Petrobras, as well as the Odebrecht engineering and construction firm, the largest in South America, whose top executive, Odebrecht family scion Marcelo, has been sentenced to 19 years in jail.

Aurelius Capital Management—the vulture fund that litigated against Argentina for years, and whose president Mark Brodsky is a protege of vulture fund kingpin Paul Singer—has been up to its eyeballs in efforts to destroy Petrobras. Just a few days after Dilma's Jan. 1, 2015 inauguration, Aurelius tried unsuccessfully to force Petrobras into default, which would have had devastating consequences for the economy. At about that time, it also began buying up Petrobras shares, as their value kept dropping, today holding an estimated five percent of the company's total shares.

Lava Jato has also targeted Brazil's Economic and

Social Development Bank (BNDES), for decades the national center for directed credit to infrastructure, as well as for many of the recent agreements signed with BRICS member China. The bank is accused of participating in bribery and corruption associated with Petrobras, and calls are already circulating for its privatization, or shutting it down altogether.

Mauro Santayana, a figure of some prominence in nationalist and socialist circles, now in his eighties, warned in a May 24 article in *Rede Brasil Atual* that *Lava Jato* is an instrument of fascism, something that neither Dilma nor other coup opponents have dared to say publicly. *Lava Jato*, he warned, is the "permanent criminalization of politics and the bringing down of all parties and public men, using 'justice' and the population which ... can only strengthen ... the fascism" which threatens the country.

Pre-War Maneuvering

The developments related here must not be viewed as either merely a fight over "economic" policy, or as simply a "timeless" commitment of Wall Street and London to fascist economic looting. Rather—as in the case of the struggle now being waged inside Japan, and the recent signs of resistance to the NATO war build-up in Germany—what we are seeing is a series of intense "theater" battles within a global strategic war.

Far from enjoying a position of unchallenged power, from which to conduct economic looting and financial speculation, the trans-Atlantic empire is facing imminent financial bankruptcy and rapid physical-economic destruction. The BRICS perspective, the Eurasian New Silk Road, and China's "One Belt, One Road" initiatives have confronted the dying trans-Atlantic world with the reality of the complete loss of global hegemony. Its response, so far, has been to take the world further down the path toward global war.

This is what Obama is doing. This is what the British are doing.

What we are witnessing in Brazil and Argentina, and the persecution—or worse—of Dilma Rousseff and Cristina Fernández de Kirchner, is just the precursor in a series of escalating attacks that threatens to take the whole world into hell. That is the lesson, and the strategic reality, which must be understood at this moment of crisis.

Every Day Counts In Today's Showdown To Save Civilization

NEW REDUCED PRICE!

That's why you need EIR's **Daily Alert Service**, a strategic overview compiled with the input of Lyndon LaRouche, and delivered to your email 5 days a week.

For example: On Jan. 7, EIR's Daily Alert featured the British hand behind the pattern of global provocations toward war. Of special note is British Intelligence's role in instigating the Saudi Kingdom's attempt to set off a Sunni-Shia war. This religious war has been the intent of British strategy since the Blair-Bush attack on Iraq in 2003.

We also uniquely update you regularly on the progress toward the release of the suppressed 28 pages of the Congressional Inquiry on 9/11, which would expose the Saudi role.

Every edition highlights the reality of the impending financial crash/bail-in policies that would realize the British goal of mass depopulation.

This is intelligence you need to act on, if we are going to survive as a nation and a species. Can you really afford to be without it?

THURSDAY, JANUARY 7, 2016

Volume 2, Number 97

EIR Daily Alert Service

P.O. BOX 17390, WASHINGTON, DC 20041-0390

- British Crown Pushing War and Genocide in 2016
- Financial Mudslide Goes On; Monetarist Tyranny Gloats over Bail-Ins
- Moody's Downgrades Portugal's Novo Banco
- Puerto Rico's Default: It's Every Vulture for Himself
- Wide Glass-Steagall Debate Set Off Again by Sanders Speech
- MI6 Mouthpiece Evans-Pritchard Touts Persian Gulf Chaos
- North Korea Tests a Miniaturized Hydrogen Bomb
- Uighur Terrorists Found in Indonesia
- Foreign Investors Are Flocking In to China

EDITORIAL

British Crown Pushing War and Genocide in 2016

II. The Future Is Now

Kra Canal: 'One of the Greatest Achievements of Modern History'

by Michael Billington

June 2—One of the truly great infrastructure projects for transforming the future of mankind, the Kra Canal, has recently been given a new and powerful impulse from several directions simultaneously. The Chinese call it the "golden waterway." It has drawn serious study and support from nations across Asia and the West. It was recently called "China's Panama Canal" by one of America's leading strategic scholars. Although it will be located in southern Thailand, it will immediately benefit all of the nations of South Asia, Southeast Asia, and East Asia, while also enhancing the economies of Europe, the Mideast, and the Americas.

http://kracanal-maritimesilkroad.com/en/

Map showing proposed site of the Kra Canal, and how it would provide an alternative to the Malacca Strait shipping choke point.

EIRNS

Lyndon LaRouche in dialogue with the audience after speaking at the EIR-*sponsored Development of the Pacific and Indian Ocean Basins conference, 1983.*

The concept of digging a canal across the Isthmus of Kra in southern Thailand, linking the Gulf of Thailand with the Andaman Sea, while also linking the entire Pacific and Indian Ocean basins, has been in men's minds since at least 1677, when Thai King Narai called on French engineers to do a survey and feasibility study. It reappeared several times in the Nineteenth Century, but ultimately the British crushed the idea in order to maintain control of the waterways in Asia through their colonial outpost in Singapore, keeping the Malacca Strait as a strategic choke point.

In the 1980s, the project was nearly successfully launched, through the effort of Thai political leaders who called upon Japan's visionary thinker, Masaki Nakajima, who headed the Mitsubishi Global Infrastructure Fund (GIF), and Lyndon LaRouche, who found in Nakajima a true partner in the idea that "Great Projects" linking nations and regions of the world, including emphatically the Kra Canal, were the necessary precondition for ending the British Empire once and for all, and introducing an era of "peace through development" based on the common good.

This collaboration, which resulted in two international conferences in Bangkok in 1983 and 1984, co-sponsored by the Thai government and LaRouche's *Executive Intelligence Review*, the magazine you are reading, could have succeeded, but for the onset of the British-run "post-industrial society" fraud and financial warfare against especially the United States and Japan. Only now, as the world is experiencing the emergence of a new paradigm, centered in China, Russia, and India, to counter the bankrupt hulk of the British Empire's European and American satrapies, is the possibility of building the Kra Canal again presenting itself to mankind.

As LaRouche said upon learning of the new developments reported here, "the building of the Kra Canal is crucial for all waters and all nations in the region, linking India and South Asia to China and the other East Asian nations. Were it to be done, it would be one of the greatest achievements of modern history."

He pointed to the importance of the fact that the near success of the project in the 1980s was the result of his close cooperation with leading forces in Japan, and that Japan is now taking steps to break away from the western war policy in favor of economic cooperation with Russia and China in the development of Asia and the world.

Two Crucial Interventions

Two events on the same day, May 30, mark the new impulse for the Kra Canal project—the leading Thai government advisory body and a leading U.S. China scholar both issued reports promoting the benefits of building the Kra Canal in southern Thailand.

Thailand's National Reform Steering Assembly (NRSA), the 200-strong advisory body on legal and developmental matters formed by Prime Minister Prayuth Chan-ocha last year, has proposed to the Prime Minister, according to the *Bangkok Post*, a networking plan to build the canal.

General Harn Leenanond, former commander of the 4th Army Region and chief project adviser, said the proposal "aims to stimulate the economies in the southern provinces, and create jobs," with "spin-off effects

Gen. Saiyud Kerdphol, former Supreme Commander of the Thai Armed Forces, shown here addressing the 1984 EIR Bangkok Conference. He is flanked by (left to right) Pakdee Tanapura of Thailand; Dr. Zainuddin Bahari of Malaysia's Institute for Strategic and Economic Studies; Dr. Norio Yamamoto of Japan; Dr. Svasti Srisukh, former Thai secretary general of the Office of Atomic Energy for Peace; K.L. Dalal, former Indian Ambassador to Thailand; and Dr. H. Roeslan Abdulgam, adviser to Indonesian President Suharto.

for the national economy." The *Post* added that the Thai-Chinese Culture and Economy Association (TCCEA), co-chaired by *EIR*'s associate in Thailand Pakdee Tanapura, together with private sector interests, have spent more than a year preparing a plan for launching the canal project, as seen on the TCCEA website, The Kra Canal—New Gateway to Maritime Silk Road. The increasing Chinese interest in the canal as part of Xi Jinping's New Maritime Silk Road has breathed new life into the concept.

Prime Minister Prayuth, asked about the proposal, repeated his policy that it is not the right time, pointing to security issues in the region. Nonetheless, the public support from the NRSA, which has representation from government, military, and royalty, and academic and private sectors, demonstrates the increasing support for the concept within the country.

The 1983 *EIR*/Thai Government conference in Bangkok, titled "The Development of the Pacific and Indian Ocean Basins," presented the Kra Canal, together with plans for construction of new deep-water ports at either end, and industrial zones in adjacent areas, as the central hub of an Asia-wide development approach, based on projects including the development of the Mekong River basin, major water control projects in China, and water and power projects in the Ganges-Brahmaputra region of India. The intention was to counter the already well-advanced collapse of the world economy into a "post industrial" junk heap and speculative bubble.

Prime Minister Prayuth rejected the immediate launching of the project on the grounds that the canal would "divide" Thailand and encourage the Muslim insurgents in the region to declare independence of the southernmost provinces. This issue had already been addressed at the 1983 conference as a failure of policy makers internationally—especially in the era of "post-industrial society" propaganda from the international financial institutions—to grasp the concept presented by Pope Paul VI in his 1968 encyclical "Populorum Progressio," that "Development is the new name for peace." In fact, the New Silk Road Economic Belt and the New Maritime Silk Road launched by Xi Jinping in 2013, as well as the Chinese-initiated Asian Infrastructure Investment Bank (AIIB), are based on precisely that principle, which President Xi identifies as "win-win," and which Helga Zepp-LaRouche refers to as the "common aims of mankind."

In this case, the Kra Canal complex, as a major industrial growth-spot, would not divide the nation, but would function as an integrating and unifying factor, joining together the southern, central, and northern provinces in a large common endeavor capable of inspiring the entire nation, uplifting the economic condition of the more impoverished southern population, and thereby reducing the potential for dissatisfaction and dissension, while also uniting all the Pacific and Indian Ocean nations around a common development hub.

Gen. Harn, who, as mentioned, presented the NRSA proposal to launch the Canal to the Prime Minister on May 30, also spoke at the *EIR* conference in Bangkok in 1984. As Commander of the southern-based Thai Fourth Army, he was known for bringing peace to the South through a process of cooperation with the local population and the promotion of development. He insisted in his presentation in 1984 that the Kra Canal was precisely what was needed to unify the population of

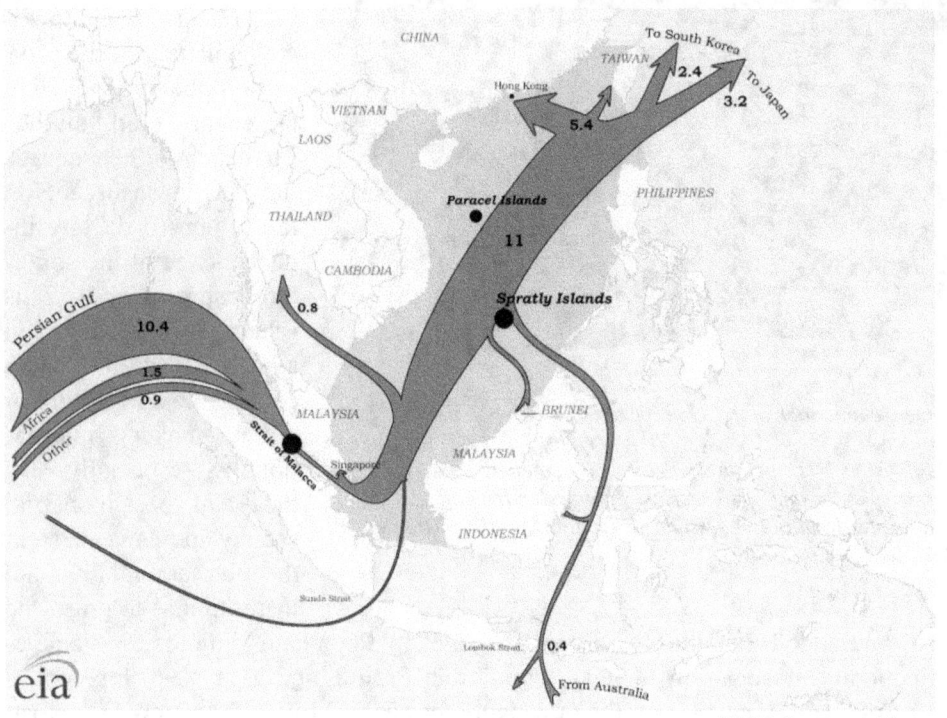

EIA/U.S. Department of Energy

The major crude oil trade flows in the South China Sea (2011), shown in millions of barrels per day, that pass through the Strait of Malacca.

at the 1984 conference in Bangkok, is still with the GIF and is collaborating with Pakdee Tanapura, promoting the project both within Thailand and at a number of conferences in China. Also in Japan, Daisuke Kotegawa, a former Ministry of Finance official and Japanese representative to the IMF who is now at the Canon Institute, has shown that the Kra Canal, as a project of great benefit to both China and Japan, is the perfect project for the collaboration of those two nations to overcome strategic tensions by joining forces with Thailand to achieve their common win-win benefit.

U.S. Strategic Scholar Presents Reality

Thailand. The 1983 and 1984 conferences presented a highly developed scheme for the Canal. A feasibility study commissioned by K.Y. Chow of the Thai Oil Refining Company was completed in 1973 by the American engineering firms Tippetts-Abbett-McCarthy-Stratton (TAMS) and Robert R. Nathan Associates, in collaboration with the U.S. Lawrence Livermore National Laboratory.

Leading representatives of all the Southeast Asian nations—with the exception of Singapore—were in attendance at one or both of the two Bangkok Conferences of 1983 and 1984. Representatives of TAMS and Lawrence Livermore travelled to Thailand to speak, and leading political and business figures from Japan and India participated. Thai Minister of Communications Samak Sundaravej opened the Conference, saying that, "If the Kra Canal is possible, then we should dedicate it to the world." A financial plan was presented by Bangkok Bank Vice President and Chief Economist Dr. Nimit Nontapunthawat.

Today, the AIIB, as well as China's $20 billion New Maritime Silk Road fund, are obvious potential sources of funding for the project. As for Japan, Dr. Norio Yamamoto who, as a deputy to Mr. Nakajima at the GIF, spoke

In the United States, Prof. Lyle Goldstein, a China scholar (and Russian scholar) at the China Maritime Studies Institute at the Naval War College, published an insightful analysis of the Kra Canal (a rarity in the United States), analyzing the increasing support for the Canal within China, under the title, "Will This Be China's Panama Canal?" Noting the dramatic economic and cultural benefits of linking the Pacific and Indian Ocean basins through the Canal, Goldstein says the Canal could become the "main act" to the "sideshow" being orchestrated by Obama in the South China Sea.

He points also to China's concern over the "Malacca dilemma," the overcrowding of traffic in the Strait of Malacca and the danger of the United States closing off the strait in a military move against China.

Goldstein takes note of the difficulties, especially the political restraints within Thailand. But he concludes, significantly: "Washington would do well to maintain an agnostic or even modestly supportive disposition toward projects that help knit Eurasian peoples and markets closer together. The Kra Canal is hardly a threat to U.S. national security and . . . is mainly an issue for the people of Thailand to decide upon."

What Makes Mankind Important?

This is an edited transcript of Lyndon LaRouche's dialogue with the Manhattan Project on June 4, 2016.

Question: This is Al K— from New Jersey. Yesterday, we received a message that an officer in the Army wrote a letter to President Obama, resigning his commission because of the savagery of the drone program … Picture it to yourself; Suppose it was you in this neighborhood. You're coming home from work; you hear a loud explosion. You come around the corner and you see that the house next to you is in rubble; lying on the ground and in flames. Your house has flames coming from the windows. The message is going back to the White House, "Mission accomplished; there is collateral damage." This is the sort of thing that is done from the White House with no danger to themselves. Don't you think this is time for the 25th Amendment to be implemented? Isn't this what it's for? Do we have to contend with barbarism and savagery?

LaRouche: Well, these considerations are of paramount importance, but they do not win on their own. We have to take that idea, the idea of what should be done, and we have to make it real. That is, we have to actually challenge Obama, for example. Now, we can do that. Putin, for example, in Europe, has done that; he's challenged Obama quite successfully.

As a matter of fact, Obama is on the fall; he's on the edge of collapse. Now, Obama could cause a great deal of harm to the population; no question about it. But, if the people of the United States and other nations decide that they're not going to give in to Obama and to what he represents, then that, in and of itself, is right to be considered as on the edge of achievement. In other words, there are certain kinds of conditions in government and elsewhere, in these kinds of matters, in which you can say, "Well, we're living in a hopeless cause."

But we're no longer in that; we are living in a deadly cause, but we're not in a hopeless one. And what we're going to have to do, is to get deeper insight into what the forces are that are necessary and are able to solve this problem. Because you'll find that with enough courage from enough citizens, we can defeat Obama and everything that he represents, and that people who like him represent. We can do it; but we're going to have to do it willfully and competently.

So, I would suggest we just start thinking about how does our mind—when working properly—how does our mind seem to accomplish miracles? They're not really miracles, but they're just the courage of people. Like in Classical music that we do in the Manhattan area—we give more and more attention to Classical musical composition and its performance on an international scale. And this is a power, because that kind of Classical musical composition, when understood effectively, is actually a force. A force which can defeat great enemies of mankind.

The Quality of Genius

Question: Good afternoon, Mr. LaRouche. This is Jessica from Brooklyn. I'm a teacher, as you and everyone here knows … My mom was a teacher, and she collected a lot of books and papers and stuff. In going through my mother's teaching materials, I came across a book published in the early 1950s by Bertrand Russell.

Bertrand Russell here smiles upon victims attending his experimental school, Beacon Hill, founded in 1927.

This book was on parenting and children. It shocked me that this book was around, and then when I thought about it, there are probably other things that the teachers were introduced to at that time … But parenting is not something that I think of Bertrand Russell as doing. He's not a child psychiatrist or psychologist; he was not a teacher in a school system or anything like that.

One of the things that stood out—and that is totally opposite to what my mom used to do with me and my two sisters—was that it said that children should not be pushed and brow-beaten into careers that may be too difficult for them. And I thought about this and what's going on in the school system now. We have a whole thing on career

Albert Einstein as a 14-year-old student in 1893.

readiness, but the careers that this Common Core system is pushing on the children are, go to college—but they're talking about community colleges. Get two years, that's enough. You don't have to get a bachelor's degree; you don't have to go four years … the aspiration to go to the higher level is kind of put down.

So, I would like you to comment on this; you once said that Bertrand Russell was the epitome of evil. And in reading this, where you don't push your children into doing anything worthwhile, because it might be too hard for their little brains to understand,— I'd like you to comment on some of the things you said about Bertrand Russell.

LaRouche: Russell was a piece of criminality with Satanic qualities. He actually induced among people who had been scientists earlier in those immediate decades,— they sold their souls out in order to get a better income. Einstein was the only man who measured up to the challenge, and that is the thing to follow. What we need to do, really, is study Einstein; he's the only one who knew what he was talking about, rightly. And therefore we should be organizing people to say, "Get that crap out of our school system. Get it out of the minds of our people; get it out of the minds of our so-called 'scientists' who ain't much in science." And build a basis by that mechanism which destroys Bertrand Russell and everything that he represents; but this

really goes to opening the gate for access to the true principles of human discovery.

Question: Hi, Lyn; it's Daniel. I have a question for you, which may or may not be related. Can genius be taught?

LaRouche: In a sense, yes. But the whole idea of genius is a quality of persons who have developed themselves to levels which are far beyond those of other people. Now if you look in the history of mankind, you can trace this kind of category of person quite well. I have enjoyed that material; I have seen the greatest achievements in terms of genius of people in their own time. I've seen implicitly and recognized that some of the greatest minds died, and there was no one to replace them. So, the question is, we have to concentrate on the idea that there has to be a standard of performance, like Einstein, and the people before him.

Shakespeare himself had a certain kind of this quality; he wasn't an Einstein, but he had a certain quality which was very useful and made possible the progress of mankind in his own time. So the question we have to concentrate on is, what are the experiences which mankind has found? Like Jeanne d'Arc, for example, a hero figure; she was murdered, she was cooked in fact, by a British crowd. But she survived in memory and became a great force in France and for France at a later point. And despite what some French politicians might say, the essence of Jeanne d'Arc still lives.

What Is the Human Mind?

Question: Good afternoon, Mr. LaRouche. I'm going to preface my question with a little bit about Chinese culture. I know that in their dealings with the world, they have a policy of not rocking the boat, you could say. So, my question is, how do you feel about the Chinese joining the IMF's Special Drawing Rights this September?

LaRouche: I don't think that China, the Chinese leadership, wants anything to do with anything that might come into connection with something like Obama, or people like that. Obama is something which

Jeanne d'Arc, France's murdered hero figure, shown here in battle. Her memory later became a great force in France.

is to be removed from the record of the human race … But the point is, mankind must actually think in terms of what we'd call a scientific principle, a social principle. And it's the ability of great scientists, great musicians, and people like that,— these are the people who inspire the advancement of mankind through the minds of individuals among mankind. And that's what you're looking for; you're looking to try to grab an idea. An idea which you can adduce; an idea which you can find in exploration. You want to see in yourself something of that creative power; you want to learn it, you want to accept it. You want to develop it, you want to preach it, you want to push it. You want to make it grow.

Just to get to the meat of the issue, what is a human mind? What is the human mind? It's a creative force when functioning; and this power, this force is a thing that makes mankind meaningful. Without this quality, mankind ain't useful. Just think of the number of citizens of the United States who seem to be surviving, seem to

have strong opinions, but it's all junk. They don't have any brain power of any merit or worth, unless we can push them into seeing what that is. *Our job is a missionary job; it's to develop in our own citizens and among other citizens as well, a process of intellectual development which is truly unique.* Not some guesstimate, but something which is precious. And you try to express what that goal is, in terms of things that you can come to understand, as being necessary.

Question: Hi, Mr. LaRouche; this is R— from Bergen County, New Jersey. We talk about a paradigm shift in moving from the "I win, you lose" old paradigm and the need to go to a new paradigm which is that we would both win. It reminded me of the early 20th Century, when Einstein published his papers [on Special Relativity] in 1905, there was a big paradigm shift in science that some people have described as a structure of scientific revolution. So it seems like we're talking about a revolution in a paradigm, bringing in a new paradigm, which I believe would be a revolution of a sort. Can you think of a previous historical time, where such a huge paradigm shift that we're talking about, has happened?

LaRouche: Yeah, sure. We've seen it in the Renaissance, the Renaissance itself. I've had a lot of experience with that in different parts of my life. It works that way! But you say, "How does this work?" That's the question.

Well, the truth of the matter is that when human beings develop, what is it that makes them develop? That's the question. Now, most people today, and in society today in most of the world, do not develop. They think they have what they call development, sometimes, but it's not development.

See the problem is this, there's this great story out there, this great fraud. The fraud is, the assumption that the human mind achieves creativity on the basis of a newborn baby. Not the parents! But the baby itself.

In other words, it's not finding some smart guy out there, that makes human history. It's when something happens, when the human mind is developed in some mysterious way, and this power is *what makes mankind important.* Mankind's existence depends upon *that particular kind of achievement.* It is not done by learning lessons, by doing this, doing that; it's a stroke of what we call "pure genius." And what you want to do, you want to find out where genius is, find out how you can use it, and teach your parents how to discover it.

Where Genius Comes From

Question: Hi Lyn, it's Chance. I've been in Germany for the last three years and it's very interesting being here in Manhattan for the various activities that we've had. One thing you've always stressed, is how do we recreate the Manhattan Project in other areas, and I've been thinking about this a lot from the standpoint of European culture. And specifically in Germany, there is a tendency to over-examine things, and to not allow a certain amount of, I guess you could say, an internal instinct, which expresses itself in Manhattan as a type of patriotism. And we noticed this on Memorial Day: We had the celebration. A lot of people were performing music; a lot of it was the American pieces. And in my mind I just imagined how it wasn't a "musical performance," it was actually a response to being an American on Memorial Day and expressing what that meant.

So my question is, how do you recreate something like that in Germany, where you have this tendency to not necessarily express that patriotism. It seems like you have...

LaRouche: [crosstalk] ... you had one of the greatest scientists in Germany [Krafft Ehricke], that is, in the course of his life; and he died, and was killed essentially, by Obama. That is, this great leader, was a creative force and there was almost *no one* like him. There were some people who approximated what he did, but he died because he had complicated diseases and conflicting kinds of diseases for which he could find no cure, so he died under those circumstances.

We now have, in the United States, in a good part of the southern states, we are taking and rebuilding that program. We're developing it. We're not groping for it.

You find the same thing in China. The leadership in China is going through a phase where in this coming period, you're going to find a quality of genius in China, in the Chinese establishment, which you would never have sought before. And when the people discover this, they're going to look at what happened in the testing of the prin-

General Dynamics Astronautics

One of 20 components of a space station, Outpost, proposed here by Krafft Ehricke in 1958.

ciple of that ... and we're going to get a second chance where ... there's going to be another great turn, coming out of China, and this development is going to be a leading force in the development of mankind in general.

That's what the truth is. And it's the same thing: You have to say, genius does not come from babies; genius comes from babies who have a *power to grow up*, to think and so forth, where others have not. And the people who are these geniuses, are the people who may enable mankind to go into the whole system and create a *new idea of the Universe. And that's what the point is.* We can do it. But you have to find the children, the geniuses, the Einsteins and people like him, and the Einsteins will give you the means to rescue the other people. And that genius is really sacred, as with Einstein.

Question: Hi, Lyn. I'm asking a question that was sent in by Avneet, who unfortunately cannot be here. So she asks the following:

"The Indian Prime Minister Modi is on his way to Washington, D.C. this week, where in a two-day visit, he will meet with President Obama and he will address a Joint Session of Congress. He is coming to the United States after visiting in Afghanistan where he is right now; and Qatar, Switzerland, and then finally he'll be in the United States.

"In a recent interview with the *Wall Street Journal*,

Prime Minister Modi maintained the non-aligned stance of his government. Given that India, in a recent brilliant move to extend the Silk Road, is helping Iran build the Chabahar Port, what do you think that Modi is coming to the United States for? And what should he expect?"

LaRouche: Well, he's not there to see Obama. [laughter] He's making the visit for what it's worth, as cheap material. He's trying to capture an idea, and get rid of Obama, or throw him out of power; that is, to point out that he is really a failure, that he's disgusting, he should never have been born, or things like that. Those are the kinds of terms.

So what we're looking at, is this idea, this wonderful idea, that there are certain babies, which are born and developed and they are born and developed in such a way that they become what we call "geniuses," like Einstein—like Einstein. And therefore, you will find that great people, in science and culture in general, will tend to lean toward the achievement of real human creativity. And that's what we're looking for: We want to find the babies who are going to be the leading agents for bringing ordinary human beings into the quality of the practice of genius.

It's Not Mysterious

Question: Hi, Lyn, this is Asuka from New Jersey. I have exactly the question on what you stated about genius, and I hope that when we look for that baby, we know what we're looking for. But I've been personally having a lot of questions about the dialogue process and the communication of ideas in society. There are a number of discussions that I have had,— unfortunately I have to characterize them as a failure in terms of conveying an idea or inspiring the other person's mind. When you look at characters such as Einstein, one thing that comes up to me, is a generation prior to Einstein, where you had the Mendelssohn family, collaborating with Humboldt, Schiller, Riemann, of course, and other great minds in Germany, who were trying to create the nation.

So, maybe if you can give us a better sense of what kind of society do we need to create, to find and generate genius?

LaRouche: All the greatest minds that I know of, in history, are of that nature... What happens is, you get a great genius, somebody becomes a genius, but it's not becoming a genius, it's that the quality of genius *infects them*. They have it, and then, if they are smart, if they are up to living to what they should be, they will express what we call "genius."

And therefore, we will use that in education, you will find great teachers are always that way. All great teachers are geniuses. And they seem to become so in various ways and various kinds of ways, but that's the way it works.

And of course, the fools do not like that. They want everybody to become El Cheapo. So don't hobnob with cheapos.

Just realize that there are people who do have a quality of genius, and they don't smudge it! They recognize a genius in themselves, and they realize that this talent which has come to them, is something which is of a very serious nature, for the benefit of mankind. It's when mankind sees himself as being a discoverer, whose work is indispensable for mankind's future, that's where the beauty comes.

Question: Good afternoon, Mr. LaRouche, this is I—. I attended a function yesterday of the Indo-Caribbean Alliance, and it was very good. Most of the people were Indo-Caribbean, but there were some black people there, and it was very good. You know, I always talk about the Caribbean, I'm pro-Caribbean; but the guest speaker said that the English-speaking Caribbean people must get together and pool our resources, so the region and those people who are living here can benefit from what is going on in America. It was very good, well received by everyone.

What I would like to know is if you have any pointers as to how those geniuses in the Caribbean who think they're from a small region can contribute towards the world?

LaRouche: I have a friend who's deceased [William Warfield], and this friend of mine was one of the greatest bass-baritones in the history of the United States. And he died, in due course. He was denied the right to have a wife, because the wife was chopped up in a sense by demanding that she do what the Met Opera does in Manhattan. And he went through a torture and she went through a torture, and they went through a life with a torture. This is the kind of thing you've got to think about! How do you ensure, that some of the greatest minds in art, and other things,— they are precious, but they are destroyed, or mauled, or manipulated, for the sake of, say, the opera in Manhattan. That kind of thing.

And what you're looking at is a kind of degeneration, a moral fault, and that's the way it is. So therefore, the question is, two things: There are factors which do account for what we call genius. Or, in time, it often comes up, a surprise, spurting out freely into society, and people are captured by it; they're infected by it, they admire people who are creative. And this is all one big picture.

But the point is, the way you have to look at this picture, you have to look at the actual role of *true genius, individual human genius.* And you have to find out where that genius lies, where you can capture it, where you can make it play, for the sake of humanity—and for the sake of *all* humanity.

No, this is not something mysterious. It's something difficult for some people to catch. I am not one of those people who cannot catch genius.

Fostering Genius

Question: Yes, good afternoon. My name is O— and I'm from Staten Island. The question I have is, and it's based on the fact that our society is tinted—tends not to link us to genius, so to speak. That's the vibe that I get. But what is the best way to search it out; what kind of environment is best at bringing out the genius in children? And how do we foster it within this American society?

LaRouche: Well, first of all, you have to have a genius in children. And you have to have a condition under which the children are energized and given access to great discovery. Now, not all children will come up to that standard. But if you don't have any children that meet that standard, then society is in a terrible condition.

What happens is, genius nurtures genius. And you want genius of some kind to educate children, to educate the people who have great skill. And you want to put it to harness, in order to say, "this person, and this person's activity, is essential for the progress of humanity." Once you see that, and think that thought, you are on the road to genius.

Question: I just want to be thankful for your genius in our generation and our century, because none of us would be here, had you not taken this course in history. And I just want to add an anecdote. I hope it's truthful. I've read it, but that doesn't mean it's true. You made the reference to infancy and genius, and the story that I discovered is that Albert Einstein never uttered a word until he was two years old. His parents took him to specialists throughout Germany, where there were some of the best specialists in the world, and studied this problem. Was there something wrong, could he not hear? He couldn't speak, what shall we do with little Albert?

So Mother brought home a surprise one day: A baby sister. And she presented the little sister to Albert, and

said, "Albert! This is your baby sister." And he spoke his first words, which were, "Where are the wheels?" It's not that obvious who our geniuses are!

LaRouche: [laughs] You got it! You're right, that's the relevant example.

Dennis Speed: I have a question for you, as a final or concluding question. There's an event that you may have heard about; and even if you didn't hear about it, I'm going to tell you about it. The fighter, Muhammad Ali, passed away today.

Now, I know that you—there was something you used to say, and it was in many of our publications in the 1970s and 1980s, that a person must use his mind like a Muhammad Ali uses his fists. Now, some of us should remember, his name was first Cassius Clay, and that in his first fight, he had changed his name and this became a great controversy. He was disliked severely for that, and then he said he wouldn't go fight in Vietnam, and he was stripped of his title. Right? And he said many things. He did say, "No Vietnamese ever called me …" and he said the n-word. But he also said, "If I'm going to die, I'll stay right here and fight my enemy, which is you."

You used to talk a lot also about Jesse Owens: We know that sometimes in sports, a message is sent. But there's something very specific which I want to say to you, Lyn, and bring up: Malcolm X recruited Muhammad Ali; you used to see Malcolm up at the Audubon Ballroom; and this whole idea of what Muhammad Ali really was, not just as an individual, but what he meant. There's a time when it's necessary to stand up and fight, and sometimes a person has limited resources. And I think, my question for you, for all of us here, because we got to stand up and fight, and some of us have limitations: So, how do we take what you've been talking about, all the last hour, this idea of genius—how do we take this, and make this, our way of fighting?

LaRouche: Well, what you're talking about essentially is an area of functioning which has an aspect like genius, but which may not be successfully defined as genius. Now, what you have then, in the mess presented to you as a result of this process, if you can get through to people who have these kinds of potentials, and if they will accept that kind of potential, then they are likely to be successful. But you can still recognize the fact that, even if they failed, what they were doing was not simply a failure; it was the need for a better development of their skills.

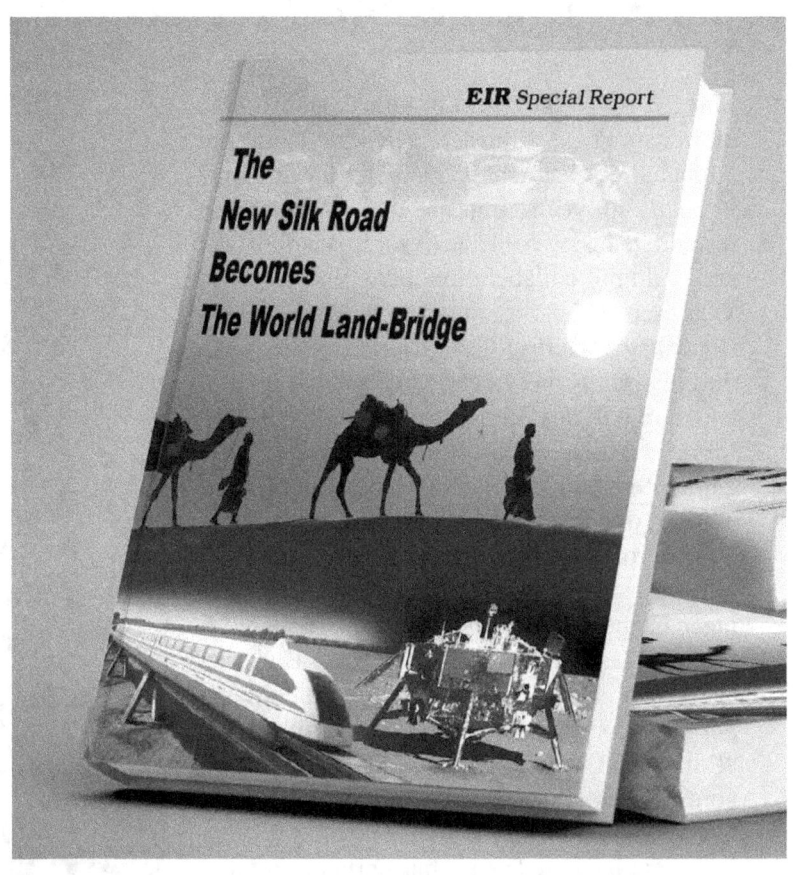

Iran at the Crossroads of The Eurasian Land-Bridge

May 27—With the recent historic visit to Tehran of Indian Prime Minister Narendra Modi and Afghan President Ashraf Ghani, for the first time in nearly 40 years, Iran has the opportunity to resume its historic role as a crossroads for trade and cultural collaboration between East and West, across the vast Eurasian landmass. *EIR*'s Copenhagen Bureau Chief Tom Gillesberg had the opportunity on March 15 to discuss Iran's potential role in this Eurasian vision with H.E. Mr. Morteza Moradian, the Ambassador of the Islamic Republic of Iran in Copenhagen, Denmark.[1] Ambassador Moradian emphasized the historic role of Iran and also the common vision of Eurasian development, which was a vital element in the talks during Chinese President Xi Jinping's visit to Iran in January 2016. "Both Iran and China have high ambitions regarding transportation issues," the Ambassador emphasized. "I think that there is extreme potential for economic development, arising from the idea raised by the Chinese President. Iran is situated at a very important juncture from a transportation point of view. This has nothing to do with the issues of today or yesterday, but it is an historical issue. Iran, and the region around it, is located along a very, very important corridor.

"If we look at the most important corridors in the world, there are three. We can see that the North-South corridor, and the East-West corridors, all pass through Iran. The important thing is that transportation corridors necessarily lead to the growth of economic development, and also, when economic development takes place, what follows is peace and stability. Our country, and all of the countries of Western Asia, are trying to

courtesy of Embassy of Iran, Copenhagen

H.E. Mr. Morteza Moradian, the Ambassador of the Islamic Republic of Iran in Copenhagen, Denmark.

find and develop these transportation routes. In this regard, the idea raised by China can have important consequences for the region. Just to sum it up, this idea of reviving the old Silk Road would have a very positive influence on development."

The Ambassador emphasized Iran's multi-modal transportation system: "Iran enjoys a very good position in regard to all forms of transportation—air, sea, and land. Iran has always followed up on the issue of reviving the old Silk Road, with China. We now see that the Chinese idea and the Iranian idea are now meeting at some point. I think that within the framework of two very important agreements, the Shanghai Cooperation

---

1. Video of the full interview, in English and Farsi, is available on the website of the Schiller Institute in Denmark, at http://schillerinstitut.dk/si/?p=12299

Organization (SCO), and also the Economic Cooperation Organization (ECO), we can have very, very good cooperation."

Russia, China, and Iran

Iran has developed strong ties to both China and Russia, and the relations among the three can be a driver for economic integration and growth, the Ambassador emphasized. "I think the conditions are now conducive for good cooperation and development. During the years of the sanctions, we had extensive relations with China. There is now about $50 billion of trade between Iran and China. This has fluctuated in some years, but it is between $50 billion and $52 billion. China is the biggest importer of Iranian oil. We also had extensive relations with Russia during the years of the sanctions. It's natural, now that the sanctions have been removed, that the relationship between these three nations would develop further.

"The important point that I would like to make is that the three countries have common interests, and common threats facing them. We are neighbors with the Russians. We have common interests with Russia regarding the Caspian Sea, transportation, energy, the environment, and peace in the world. So we have quite a number of areas where our interests coincide. Other areas where we have common interests are drug trafficking and other forms of smuggling, and combating extremism and terrorism.

"We also have quite a number of common interests with China. They include energy, reviving the Silk Road, combating terrorism, the transportation corridors, and, also, in the framework of the SCO—quite a number of areas where we have common interests. China needs 9 million barrels of oil on a daily basis. As I said, our trade relations amount to about $52 billion.

"Iran enjoys some very important advantages. First of all, it has enormous amounts of energy resources. Its coastline, along the Persian Gulf, runs 3,000 kilometers. We are neighbors with 15 countries in the region. I think that cooperation between these three powers, namely Russia, China, and Iran, can ultimately lead to stability and peace in the region. So the four areas—the combination of economics, trade, energy, and transit—these are areas that can lead to the goals that I mentioned.

"The revival of the old Silk Road, at this juncture of time, would be very meaningful. During the recent visit to Iran by the Chinese President, the two sides agreed to increase the volume of trade between the two countries, in the next ten years, to $600 billion.

"Also, in the recent visit to Iran by President Putin, there was agreement on Russian investment in Iran. It has to be said that our trade relations, economic relations, with Russia are not as great as they should be. But among the topics discussed when President Putin visited Iran, was making sure that the volume of economic cooperation increases between Iran and Russia."

Ambassador Moradian noted that the arrival of the first freight train in Tehran from China, in February, further underscored the potential arising from Iran-China collaboration on the Silk Road program. "President Rouhani has very clear views on the Silk Road. In fact, President Rouhani is a specialist in transportation routes and communication. He believes that the basis for development lies in the development of transportation infrastructure. He and the Chinese President have talked over the revival of the Silk Road on a number of occasions."

The Ambassador sharply criticized the efforts of Washington to bypass Iran in any Eurasian development plans: "There was a discussion ... being propagated during the past few years—the idea of the new Silk Road, or the American Silk Road, so to speak. Basically, they wanted to bypass Iran, and divert the route. No one can fight against economic and geographical realities on the ground. The route through Iran is the shortest route, and the cost-effective route, and, therefore, nobody can go against that. And because the Chinese ideas were more realistic, Iran and China were able to come to some sort of understanding on the development and revival of the Silk Road.

"There is also emphasis on the development of sea routes. We witnessed good investment by the Chinese in this regard, in the recent years. China has invested heavily in Pakistan, in the Gwadar port."

Transport Corridors to Defeat War

The Ambassador next turned to the immediate prospects of building the East-West and North-South transport corridors, linking Iran to Central Asia, and creating the opportunity to bring stability back to Afghanistan after more than 30 years of continual war.

"The railroad between Khaf in Iran, and Herat and

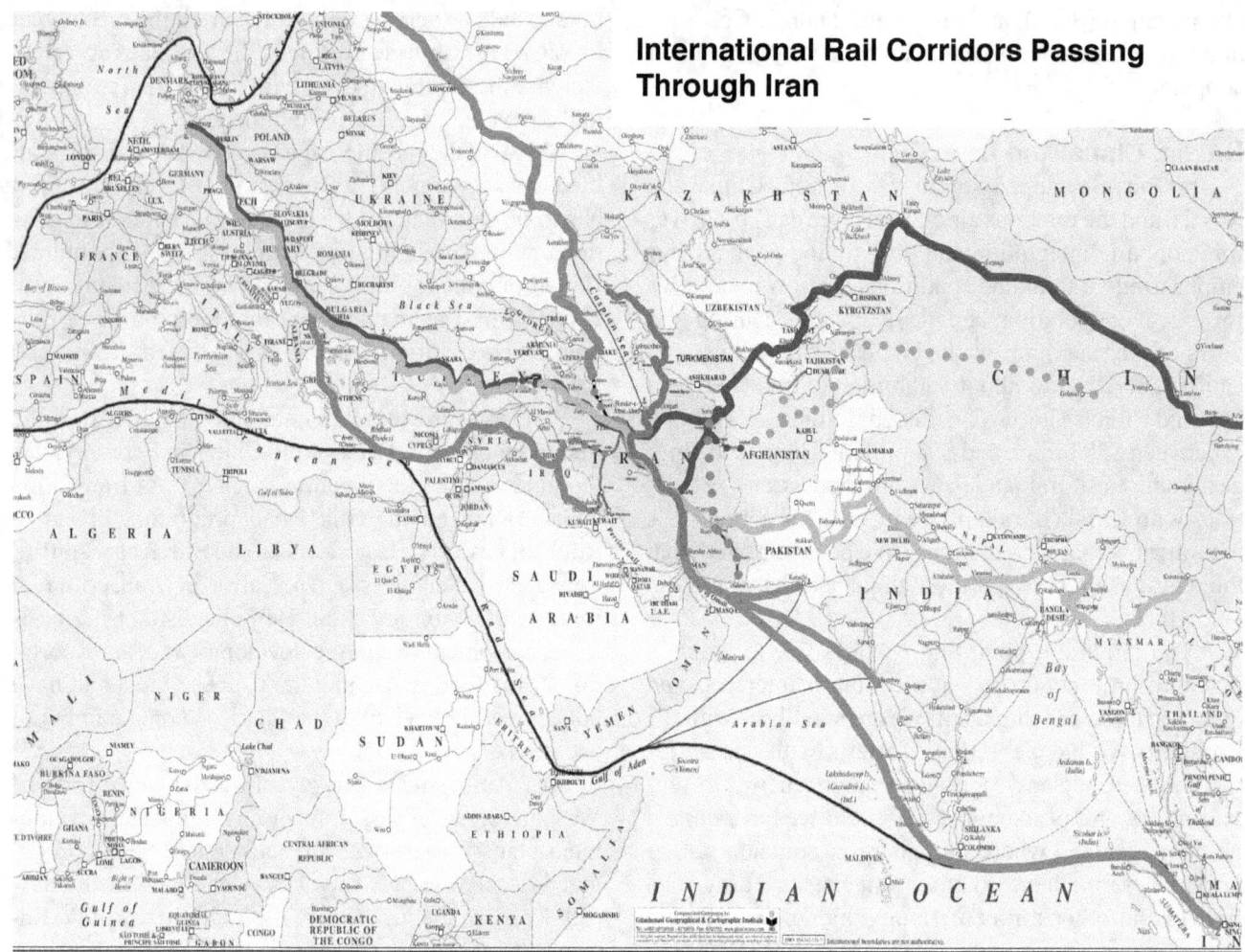

International Rail Corridors Passing Through Iran

Mazar-i-Sharif in Afghanistan, is an important connection. The Khaf-Herat section has been completed, but the Herat-Mazar-i-Sharif section is still to be constructed. I think this is an important route that we believe, in my opinion, China would be advised to invest in.

"If this route between Herat and Mazar-i-Sharif were to be completed, then from there, there are two routes—one leading to Uzbekistan and the other leading to Tajikistan, and that can be an important connection. At the moment, China is making good investments in both Kyrgyzstan and Tajikistan, to establish the links. In fact, the link connecting China, Kyrgyzstan, Tajikistan, Afghanistan, and Iran is one of the most important links of the Silk Road. And there is a missing link between Herat and Mazar-i-Sharif, as I said, and I hope that the countries concerned, especially China, can help establish that link. Over the past

two years, the corridor between Kazakstan, Turkmenistan, and Iran has borne fruit, and is now connected. In fact, the train that arrived in Teheran actually came through this route, and this corridor has extreme potential. I hear that quite a number of countries in the region are interested in joining this corridor. We have another corridor linking Uzbekistan, Turkmenistan, Iran, and Oman, which is called the fourth corridor. And this has also come into operation over the past year-and-a-half.

"We also have other corridors, which I call subsidiary corridors. All of these subsidiary corridors can actually enhance and complement the main East-West Silk Road. One very important corridor that you are aware of, is the North-South corridor, and a section along this corridor is now under construction—the connection between the city of Rasht, and Astara on the Caspian coast. In fact, we have reached agree-

North-South Corridor Passing Through Iran

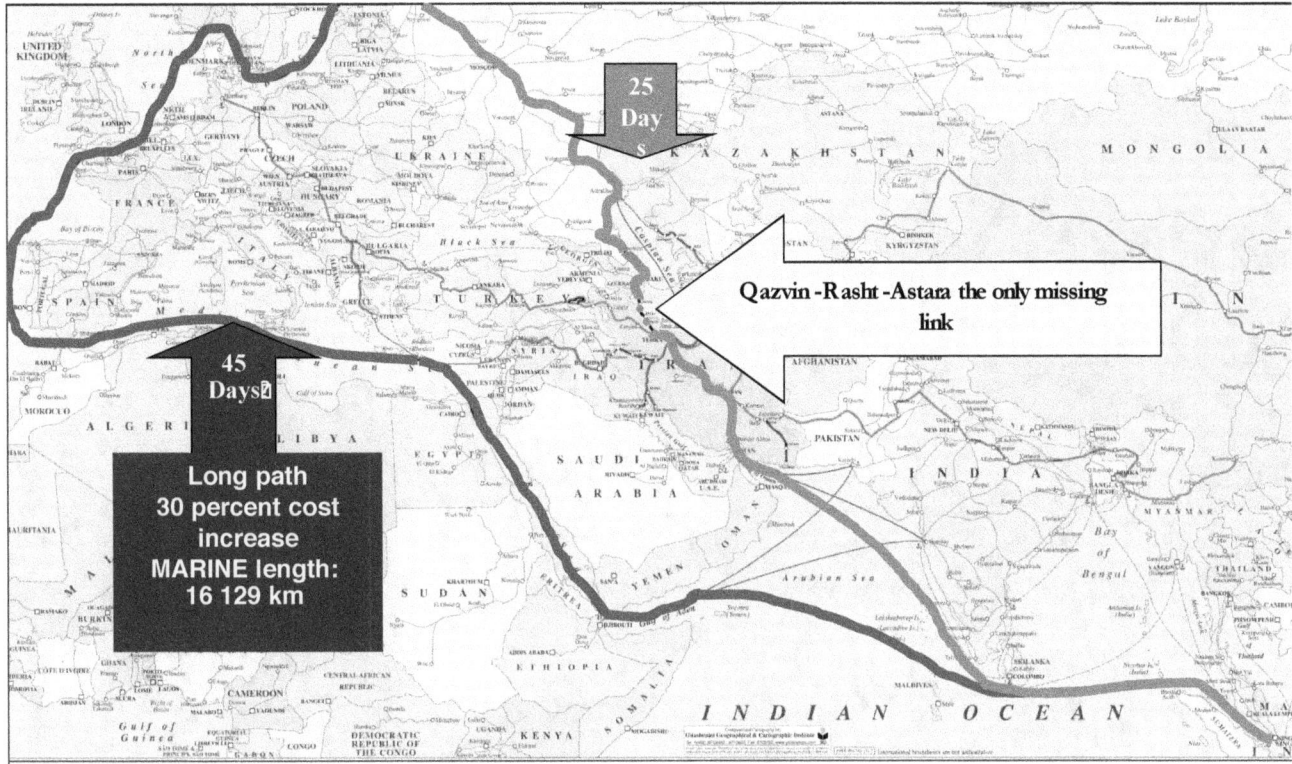

25 Days

Qazvin-Rasht-Astara the only missing link

45 Days

Long path
30 percent cost increase
MARINE length:
16 129 km

ment with Azerbaijan on the connection between the two cities of Rasht in Iran, and Astara in Azerbaijan. This corridor also needs some investment, and we hope that countries like China can help us in developing this."

The Ambassador noted that "17 agreements were signed during the visit" of President Xi Jinping to Iran in January. "The areas included energy, financial investment, communication, science, the environment, and know-how. Specifically, on the core of the Silk Road, the two countries agreed to play a leading, and a key role, in the development and operation of this link. They agreed to have cooperation on infrastructure, both railroad and road. For example, electrification of the railroad link between Teheran and Mashhad, is part of this connection of the Silk Road that was agreed to. The other important thing is cooperation on the Port of Chabahar in Iran. The two sides agreed to cooperate in this, and the Chinese agreed to invest in Chabahar. Regarding industry and other production areas, they agreed that China would cooperate and invest in twenty areas. Regarding tourism and cultural cooperation, the two sides also agreed to develop cooperation in this regard,

within the framework of the Silk Road. I think you can see that within the framework of the Silk Road, there are quite important agreements between the two countries."

Nuclear Energy Is Vital

Another vital area in which cooperation among Iran, Russia, and China is increasing, is energy, the Ambassador noted. He emphasized the role that Russia played in the completion of Iran's nuclear power plant at Bushehr: "Because of the reneging of the Western governments, the construction of the Bushehr nuclear power plant was left unfinished, and after the Russians agreed to pick up the pieces, we reached an agreement, and were able to develop, and make this very important plant operational. The cooperation between Iran and Russia on peaceful nuclear energy has been very constructive. All of Iran's atomic activities have been under the supervision of the International Atomic Energy Agency (IAEA). As we have had no deviation from our peaceful nuclear program, after ten or twelve years, the Western countries, the P5+1, finally came to the conclusion that Iran's nu-

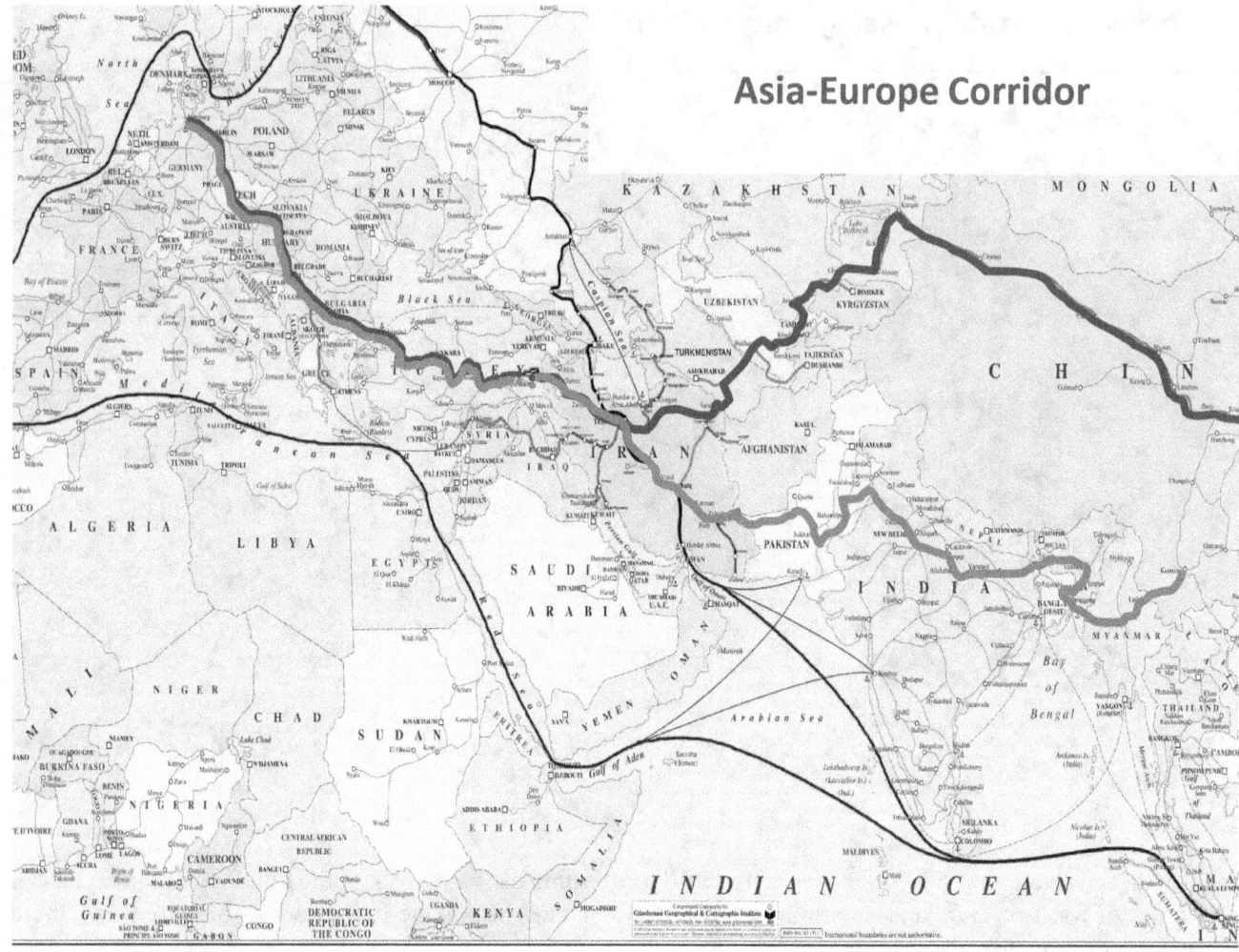

clear program has always been peaceful. I believe that they knew this at the beginning, as well. This was just a political game. "We have also had a sort of constructive cooperation with China over the past two decades on peaceful nuclear energy. During the recent visit to Iran by the Chinese President, an agreement was also signed in this regard. In the implementation of the P5+1 agreement, China, Iran, and America are also the three countries forming the committee for the implementation of the agreement. It was agreed during the recent visit that China will reconfigure the Arak heavy water plant. The Chinese and the Iranians have also agreed to cooperate on the building of small-scale nuclear power plants. This, I think, is very important for Iran, in terms of producing electricity, and the Chinese welcome this.

"We have also signed a number of agreements with China on the construction of a number of nuclear power plants in the past. Iran, because of the large extent of the country, has always welcomed cooperation in the development of peaceful nuclear energy for the production of electricity, and other things. In fact, based on the cooperation agreement between Iran and the P5+1, there will be agreements with a number of the members of the P5+1 regarding the nuclear issue."

Expanding Rail Grid

The Ambassador turned next to Iran's internal transport infrastructure needs and progress. "Iran has made endeavors, extensive efforts, to actually complete what I call the subsidiary corridors. Right now in Iran, we have 10,000 kilometers of operational railroad lines. For our present government, the further development of railroad links is very important. We have plans to build another 10,000 kilometers in the future. It is my view that in the next couple of years, we will see a revolution in transportation.

"There are some missing links, which we think

should be completed as soon as possible. We have the link to the Chabahar Port. If this port is developed to utilize its full capacity, then this will serve as an important link in the North-South corridor. In the Persian Gulf we also have an island called Qeshm, which has great potential. In fact, because Qeshm itself also has gas, and has a strategic location in the Persian Gulf, it can play an important role in the North-South corridor. We are seeing that various countries such as China, Japan, and South Korea are interested in entering into these areas." The Ambassador added that progress is also significant on the East-West corridor, where some very important developments have taken place. "We have had good negotiations with the Turkish side. One of the most important links in the East-West corridor is the link between the cities of Sarakhs and Sero. Sero is located on the border with Turkey, and the Turks and the Iranians are now in very extensive negotiations to develop this route. The other route is the railway link between Iran and Iraq, and this is also being built on an extensive level. As I said, the subsidiary corridors—the one connecting Kazakhstan, Turkmenistan, and Iran; and the one connecting Uzbekistan, Turkmenistan, Iran, and Oman—are now operational, and we are also planning on developing and making other subsidiary routes operational."

The Water Crisis

Turning next to one of the great challenges facing Iran, Ambassador Moradian acknowledged that "Iran is faced with a shortage of water." Work is underway to tackle this crucial problem, he said. "We have quite a number of projects for water desalination on the Persian Gulf. In fact, one of the main reasons that we wanted nuclear power plants on the Persian Gulf was to use that energy to desalinate water. Currently, a number of Iranian companies are engaged in this. One of the very big projects has come on stream during the past couple of years. Regarding the desalination plants, there is good cooperation between Iran and foreign countries. I think that this is another area where Danish companies can enter into the competition. President Rouhani made a trip to the city of Yazd, in the center of Iran, and he said there, that transfer of water from the Persian Gulf to the center of Iran, to the city of Yazd, is one of the important projects that the government has in mind.

"Regarding nuclear fuel, the framework of the P5+1 agreement with Iran envisages extensive cooperation between Iran and these countries on nuclear fuel. Iran is now one of the countries that have the legal right to enrich uranium, and this has been recognized. So, based on the capacities that Iran has, we can exchange nuclear fuel. Within this framework, we have exchanged quite a lot of fuel with the Russians, and we have cooperation plans with China on the heavy water plant in Arak."

SCO and the War on Terrorism

No discussion about the Greater Middle East and Persian Gulf can ignore the threat posed by terrorism and the flow of illegal drugs across borders, to markets in Europe and beyond. Ambassador Moradian was blunt: "On the issues of combating extremism and terrorism, and trafficking of drugs, there are extensive grounds for cooperation. The development of extremism, and the instability that follows, is extensive in the CIS countries, and part of China. Iran has extensive experience and knowledge about combating terrorism, and in this regard, Iran can cooperate with those countries regarding this menace. Afghanistan is the world's biggest producer of opium. In fact, unfortunately, after Afghanistan was occupied by the ISAF coalition, led by America, the level of production of opium in Afghanistan has increased greatly.

"In Helmand, in particular, there was an incredible increase in the amount of production. In fact, in combating drug smuggling into Iran, Iran has been a sturdy wall, and we have unfortunately lost quite a number of our security forces in that region, close to 4,000. In fact, Iran is on the frontline in combating drugs. When Europe talks about helping other countries stem the tide of immigrants to Europe, I think that stemming the tide of narcotic drugs coming to Europe, also requires the same sort of agreements. "There already exists very good cooperation between Iran, China, and Russia on combating drug trafficking. We have had multilateral sessions in this field. I think that within the framework of the Shanghai Cooperation Organization (SCO), Iran can play a leading role in combating drug trafficking, extremism, and terrorism. In the recent session of the SCO, it was agreed that after the sanctions were lifted against Iran, Iran's status would be elevated from an observer to a full member. In the next session, which is planned to take place in Uzbekistan, I think that this issue will be raised.

"Iran's full membership in the SCO is important. In fact, in the area of security, SCO needs Iran's experience and influence."

EDITORIAL

TOWARD A NEW GALACTIC MAN

Krafft Ehricke's Polyglobal World Now Being Realized

by Kesha Rogers

Kesha Rogers in Houston, Texas, is a leader of the LaRouche Political Action Committee and leads a campaign to revive the U.S. Space Program.

June 3—The closed world system with its "limits to growth," which rejects the creative mind of the human being and confines mankind to a state of enslavement, starvation, and war,— that system is in its death agony. Now the world is moving into a new awakening of human progress through peaceful development and cooperation among nations, guided by the leadership of nations such as Russia and China. This battle for development and scientific progress has been waged for many decades through the work of Lyndon LaRouche and Helga Zepp-LaRouche. This is the progress that the enemies of mankind, the British Empire—the promoters of population reduction—continue to despise. They can build nothing, create nothing,— they can only destroy. Now they are moving through their puppet Obama for total war and annihilation.

To understand the power that we have as human beings to defy this threat to our very existence, we must come to recognize the unique nature of our species as

EIRNS/Stuart Lewis

Space scientist Krafft Ehricke addressing a 1981 meeting.

completely distinct from the animals, in having unlimited potential through creative thought. We shall turn to the inspiration of the philosophy and scientific principles of the great German space pioneer Krafft Ehricke (1917-1984), who defined the principles of an open world system and a polyglobal civilization based on the rejection of "limits to growth."

Russia and China are leading the planet in the realization of this open world system, as defined by Ehricke, one that is coming into alignment with the increasing drive for development and cooperation. The nations of the world joining in this effort toward progress—and in what China's President Xi Jinping declared as a principle of win-win cooperation for all nations—are now transcending the confines of one globe and becoming truly polyglobal.

Ehricke's conceptions of scientific and technological progress were not confined to one nation or people, but were the very principles which govern mankind's understanding of the Universe. Ehricke's principles followed the path of the conception of "Mind" that was defined by the great astronomer and scientist Johannes Kepler (1571-1630), who discovered that the

Saturn · Jupiter · Mars, nearly · The Earth

Venus · Mercury · Here the Moon also has a place.

Johannes Kepler.

Right: Geometrical model of the solar system as nested Platonic solids, from "Mysterium Cosmographicum." Above: Harmonic relations of the planets expressed in musical notation, from "The Harmony of the World."

Kepler's discovery of universal gravitation, using principles of both visual and musical harmony, has nothing to do with the "Titius-Bode law."

Fidelio

Universe and Solar System in which we live are not a fixed system. The motions of the planets must be seen from the standpoint of a great conductor guiding an orchestra. The planets do not move without a mover, without a Mind to move them. Kepler's investigation into the motions of the heavenly bodies provided humanity's greatest-ever breakthrough in our understanding of the Universe. Kepler's discovery of the Solar System was made through the recognition of paradoxes present in the mind's eye. And similarly, the ability of mankind to travel out into our Solar System and beyond, both by leaving the Earth to travel in spaceships, and by sending instruments, requires one principle: *Mind.*

Kepler knew well that some day mankind would traverse the Solar System: "Ships and sails proper for the heavenly air should be fashioned. Then there will also be people who do not shrink for the dreary vastness of space."

Kepler looked into the future of mankind's presence in space and foreshadowed the principles for space exploration that mankind would later bring into being.

"As soon as somebody demonstrates the art of flying, settlers from our species of man will not be lacking [on the Moon and Jupiter]. Who would have believed that a huge ocean could be crossed more peacefully and safely than the the narrow expanse of the Adriatic, the Baltic Sea, or the English Channel? Provide ships or sails adapted to the heavenly breezes, and there will be some who will not fear even that void [of space]. So, for those who will come shortly to attempt this journey, let us establish the astronomy: Galileo, you of Jupiter, I of the Moon."

Krafft Ehricke's Vision

German space pioneer Krafft Ehricke knew from Kepler that it was mankind's extraterrestrial imperative to travel in space, and that only the creative mind of man, removing all limitations, could fulfill that destiny. Ehricke developed three fundamental laws to serve as the basis for mankind to fulfill our imperative for exploring space, while rejecting the prison of a closed world system, confined to limited resources.

First Law: *Nobody and nothing under the natural*

laws of this universe impose limitations on man except man himself.

Second Law: *Not only the Earth, but the entire Solar System, and as much of the Universe as he can reach under the laws of nature, are man's rightful field of activity.*

Third Law: *By expanding through the Universe, man fulfills his destiny as an element of life, endowed with the power of reason and the wisdom of the moral law within himself.*

In one of Ehricke's major works, the posthumous "Lunar Industrialization and Settlement—Birth of Polyglobal Civilization,"[1] he set out to "summarize major aspects of lunar industrialization and settlement. It identifies scientific and evolutionary facts leading to a definitive justification for why man must industrialize space, changing our present closed world into an open world." He establishes the philosophy of "The Extraterrestrial Imperative" as a "definitive justification for a

long-term future based on mankind's ability to transcend the limits of one small planet." He goes on to define what he calls "information metabolism," which is the ability of the mind of man to discover and apply new scientific principles, the capability that makes our world an open world, rather than a closed or fixed environment. Ehricke writes, "In an open world system there are no limits to growth. By capability and design, information metabolism can resolve the conflict that every umbilical metabolism has with the old environment. It can transcend the confines of one globe and become polyglobal. It has absolutely everything it needs to create a new and larger sphere of integration. I call this the androsphere."

As we break through any and all limits placed on mankind, and expand out into the far reaches of space, China's mission—to land on the far side of the Moon in the next two years and explore it, as a new leap for mankind—puts us closer to our destiny of realizing the creative principles and the Extraterrestrial Imperative of our species that Krafft Ehricke so remarkably understood. These are the principles that must govern our future—mankind must free itself from any lower intention.

---

1. Krafft A. Ehricke, "Lunar Industrialization and Settlement—Birth of Polyglobal Civilization," in: W.W. Mendell, ed., *Lunar Bases and Space Activities of the 21st Century.* Houston: Lunar and Planetary Institute, 1985, pp. 827-856. Available online at: http://adsabs.harvard.edu/full/1985lbsa..conf..827E